OLD INERTIA AND NEW TECHNOLOGIES:

LIVING IN A FAST WORLD

SERGE PLATA

ILLUSTRATIONS AND ARTWORK BY NELLY SUGAR

Bibliographic information about this book can be found at **claphampublishing.com.**

The graphic design of this book was done by Nelly Sugar and Clapham Publishing
Services, a subsidiary of Claret Press.

The illustration on the cover is a reproduction of a work entitled "Inertia and Technology" by Nelly Sugar. Nelly Sugar ©2024. For a complete reference: Sugar, N., (2024), Inertia And Technology, generated with the assistance of AI, OpenAI, London

ISBN: 978-1-7392031-2-2
©Serge Plata, 2024
14 Burnett Square, Hertford, Hertfordshire, England

TABLE OF CONTENTS

ABOUT THE AUTHOR

Serge Plata obtained his PhD in the mathematics department at Imperial College London, an EMPA at Harvard Business School and was awarded a fellowship at the Institute of Mathematics and its Applications in the UK. He is a chartered mathematician (Royal Charter) and a chartered scientist (UK Science Council) in the UK. He is author of *Visions of Applied Mathematics* (Peter Lang, 2007) as well as papers, articles and editorials for specialist magazines. He has been keynote speaker at data and technology events and academic conferences in the UK and abroad. He is a certified six-sigma black belt and he has held directorship and leadership level roles in data and decision science for businesses, AI, analytics and R&D from FTSE 100 and S&P 500 companies to startups and also international management & technology consultancies.

ABOUT THE ILLUSTRATOR

Nelly Sugar is a professional photographer and visual designer. She received her Bachelor in Arts Honours degree from University of Chester, trained in art in Florence, Italy and has traveled the world in photographic tours capturing amazing landscapes and unique portraits. Her work has been used internationally for covers of books and has appeared in art and photography publications.

ACKNOWLEDGMENTS

I would like to thank:

My dear friend Maxi Zattera who always challenges me in the best way possible, for his valuable continuous intellectual contributions and innovative ideas.

Jovana Ioannou, who has the ability to see things that I do not, and for being so generous with her thoughts and ideas.

Alec Boere for his time and patience in discussing ideas and concepts with me.

As always, Dr. Claudio Canaparo for his unconditional help, support, mentoring and formation throughout the years.

Specially, I would like to thank my amazing editor Dr. Katie Isbester for her support, ideas and outstanding work, and to her creative designer Petya Tsankova for her contribution to this book.

INTRODUCTION

Inertia: /ɪˈnəːʃə/ noun 1. A tendency to do nothing or to remain unchanged. 2. PHYSICS a property of matter by which it continues in its existing state of rest or uniform motion in a straight line, unless that state is changed by an external force.

Technology /tɛkˈnɒlədʒi/ noun 1. the application of scientific knowledge for practical purposes, especially in industry. 2. machinery and equipment developed from the application of scientific knowledge. 3. the branch of knowledge dealing with engineering or applied sciences.

This book is about both. It is a coupling that is inherently problematic. On the one hand, there's the power of inertia, that is, the weight of tradition and well accepted ideas. And on the other, there's the power of technology, that is, new scientific developments. Inertia and technology butt heads. They influence, inform and shape each other in a complex and unpredictable dynamic. And we live our lives navigating between them. We need a map, a better understanding to explore how these two phenomena interact and how we change accordingly.

The book has the philosophical view of hedonism as an axis, so by reading this book you will realize behaviours that might be convenient to change, but most importantly will help understand and make decisions in the fast world we are living in to have more pleasure than pain in life.

This work is also the juxtaposition of two views: the first is technical, which covers data and analysis and other subtleties necessary to have a decent level of discussion on technology, and the second is the strategic, business, social and human aspects of our existence which relates directly to decision making.

This book covers business applications and other strategic points that we must be aware of – and even embrace – if we want to cope with the development of new technologies. And it covers from many angles how technology is affecting our own traditional way of thinking and seeing the world.

This book has the format of a collection of short stories. In this way the book is more episodic than a well ordered thematic structured work, hence the book can be read in any order the reader wishes. However, I refer to other chapters to enhance and connect ideas and to show that the epistemology, general thesis and argument in this book is internally consistent.

Not only would executives benefit from these ideas and views in order to make better decisions involving technology, but so too would the general public to deal and cope with the modern technological world and the speed at which it is changing. While ideas are inherently persuasive – or we wouldn't have any technology at all – I suggest that ideas in this book have practical applications on daily lives and activities.

I use terms like "ecology" or "critical thinking" that deserve an entire book to be treated and developed, but for space and length reasons I refer them as general notions which suffice for the purposes of the book; I encourage the reader to also research about these topics and all the concepts exposed in this book, especially when the technology to do it is available for almost anyone on our personal devices like mobile phones.

However there are terms that I specifically define as they are crucial for the purpose of the book, for example, when tackling issues like responsible AI we need to first decide what those issues actually are: technical, scientific or technological, which furthers the importance of clearly distinguishing between terms. Our understanding of these terms will shape our engagement and response. Consequently, I take a precise perspective and definition on terms, discussing them in a separate chapter.

One of the most important points of this book is to show a fresh and rather unorthodox point of view into data, science and technology, and how this perspective will impact the way we see the world, or at least the way we should start seeing it.

Inertia and resistance to change is one of the factors dealing with the usage and spread of modern technology so in every chapter (or episode) there is a comparison of views: the traditional versus the modern. At the very least I offer examples of how the traditional views or inertia no longer work in a fast-changing technological world.

As a disclaimer, I studied science and mathematics, not philosophy, and stumble across the ideas of philosophers in a less-than-coherent manner. I have no doubt that there are other writers who arrived at the same universal truths besides the ones I have quoted, and equally that other cultures have done the same. It is both the gift of humanity that we can think and learn and share our learning with others, and the curse of humanity that we have to keep reinventing that wheel.

In addition, all that is in this book is my opinion. Many people might agree with it and others not. If you do not agree with my opinions, that is fine. Please write your own book to counter my views.

Finally, I want to point out that each chapter has unique artwork designed and created by avant-garde artist Nelly Sugar, using technology tools like ChaptGPT. Each piece of art was designed for the specific topic in each chapter, and the technology used was purposely chosen to reflect the book's theme of technology and how we are changing – even artists – with it.

Serge Plata
February 2024

CHAPTER 1.
Artificial Intelligence, What Do We Mean By That?

It is one thing to be clever and another to be wise.

George R.R. Martin

Underlying technology is human intelligence. No brains, no bytes. So the first thing we need to talk about is what intelligence is. In the 1980s there was a theory about the types of intelligence: emotional intelligence, musical intelligence, sporting intelligence, and so on. It was a long list. In all honesty I never understood the theory. I think that some of these so-called intelligence types are in fact skills different from intelligence.

I guess I am among the critics of the theory, mainly because of its subjectivity and arbitrary definitions that in the end lead to contradictions. In comparison, in mathematics we have arbitrary definitions but they are consistent within themselves and within their theory. Hence the power of axioms in mathematics. In this case, I think a definition of Intelligence should involve intellect, or the way of thinking, and this should be a good approach to intelligence leading to a consistent theory.

As this book will touch on hedonism, I would like to define intelligence in that view, for me the best way to define it is through people's behaviors, so I would summarize in this way: intelligent people have difficult pleasures.

Artificial Intelligence or AI has been defined in many ways, too many ways. We have definitions involving "technology that enables computers and to learn…" Well, using the word "learn" leads us down a rabbit hole of centuries of attempts to define it.

It has been defined as "the ability", "the simulation", "science", "engineering", "the intelligence" (this last one is using the word intelligence to define intelligence!), and so on.

Even the G20 Digital Economy Task Force had some definitions that were not precise. For example, the Eurostat definition of artificial intelligence: "AI systems can be purely software based" or Statistics Canada which defines artificial intelligence as "systems that display intelligent behavior", again defining intelligence with the word intelligence. Or Japan that defines AI as "something". See [G20 Notes, 2021].

AI is not about autonomous decisions or learning. It is not about machines. Or only about technologies. It is instead about an integrated system.

Artificial intelligence is an ecosystem of people, tools and methods to recognize patterns, establish redundancies and calculate probabilities in order to:

1) Complete incomplete sequences, in other words join the dots between scattered or separate information or data
2) Reformulate statements to solve problems
3) Automate to accelerate outcomes

This is a familiar definition of artificial AI. Once again we are repeating the old data science mantra from years ago: "tools, people and processes".

But this is only half of the definition. It is the inertial part of the definition. The modernization of it is to recognize that these three interact to create an ecosystem, and a good definition states how these parts relate to each other to achieve the three main goals above.

Bear in mind this definition as it can be connected to other chapters in the book because it is consistent with its argument and thesis.

Artificial intelligence is an ecosystem that involves humans too. It is composed of tools and processes, and it is based on machine learning techniques, which in turn are based on mathematical models and computational solutions. On the human side, the measure of intelligence is summarize as "intelligent people have difficult pleasures

CHAPTER 2.
The Way We Analyse Data

Life is neither good or bad,
but only a place for good and bad.

Marcus Aurelius

I always tell my teams that when dealing with data and drawing insights out of it, we play a "detective role", where even the lack of information is giving away valuable insights.

For example, if a customer on an e-commerce website leaves many fields blank when registering, it sends a message of either not being engaged with the brand or of too many questions asked. Further narrowing of other options can be made by cross referencing other data, like number of visits, click-throughs on emails, etc. This can determine with some degree of confidence which of our assumptions is correct.

But do blanks in the data (what we call missing data) constitute bad data? Let's first answer the question of what bad data is in a business context.

Start with the notion of *bad data*. I do not think there is bad data as such. All data is just data and the nature of it comes direct-ly from the person or organisation that creates it. Inevitably in business, data is also a reflection of the company policies, pro-cesses (even the broken ones) and culture.

The company exists and naturally produces information and all these circumstances surrounding it are reflected in its data, so the data is not the bad actor. Imagine an e-commerce retailer that noticed the sales of one of their products was decreasing rapidly with no apparent market reason for it, e.g. seasonality. On further investigation, they realized that the processes to record stock were not followed properly. This triggered a false signal to customers, making them believe that the item was out of stock and hence not buying it and hence the result in sales decreasing.

In this case, bad data is a reflection of the company's own inefficiencies. In general, there are four cases of *bad data*:

- Duplicate data
- Missing data
- Wrong data
- Misplaced data

Data is not only about the market or commercial performance of the company, but is also the reflection of internal deficiencies. Then *bad data* is also *good data,* that is, data is making us aware of situations within the company.

In data science the unspoken rule is that anything that can happen with data will happen. No dataset is perfect. We have duplicate data, missing data, null data, outliers, anomalies and errors of all sorts to the extent that we have to ask our data scientists to repair and give us a "clean" dataset to work with and make decisions.

In the best case, a data science textbook exercise that we can find in popular courses asks us to first clean the data EDA[1], then build a model (train and test sets), then draw conclusions based on metrics like accuracy, recall, precision, F1 scores, mean square errors or R-squared, that most of the time do not relate to the actual problem at hand. For metrics that make sense see [Plata, Rackiewicz, 2022].

---

1   EDA means Exploratory Data Analysis

The situation is that mostly these decisions are based or backed by an expert who has many years' experience in the field (a Subject Matter Expert or SME) and, if there is any discrepancy, would have to adjust and revise models and data until a consensus is reached. Is this really an analytic breakthrough?

The answer is no, absolutely not. This is because we still rely on human expertise and this will not change until we understand that *bad data* also gives us precious information that we ignore and conceal with the data "cleaning" exercise.

Moreover, making decisions based on clean data is – in a way – supporting all our rationale in a fiction: an ideal-made-up-world that actually does not exist in real life.

In conclusion, having "clean data" is just deceiving and not reflecting the reality of the business or situation. With modern techniques like neural networks, it is possible to feed algorithms with "bad data" and get better insights than cleaning it arbitrarily so we can run a machine-learning model.

The lessons that we obtain out of bad data are numerous and can be exploited if not being ignored.

Don't ask data teams to clean data to run a model. Better ask them to understand the data and the system that generates it. By performing the "detective work", humans will have a better understanding of the system, improve business outcomes and deal with real problems rather than perform textbook exercises that do not lead to anything practical. There is no such thing as bad data! Even the so-called bad data is good data from which we can draw meaningful insights.

CHAPTER 3.
The Way We Classify Data

Science is the systematic classification of experience.

George Henry Lewes

Due to advancements in techniques like GenAI, cloud platforms and data engineering tools, problems like "big data" are irrelevant now. When we hear people saying, "We solve big data problems," or "We need a candidate that can deal with big data," they are still thinking like everyone did ten or fifteen years ago, when managing huge amounts of data was a problem.

With modern tools this is not a problem anymore. In the old days we used to talk about continuous data, categorical data, big data, unstructured data, etc. But with GenAI, unstructured data is actually a problem that can be solved by almost anyone with no technical background.

Categorical or continuous data falls into the same kind of solutions, and even big data is a thing of the past, although we keep using and changing the definition of "big data", which sounds very convenient, right?

So the situation I observed with these new technologies is that data is more complex than before. For example, we have the so-called embedding or vectors, which sometimes are arrays of 1,500 numbers that are practically unintelligible. Taking a step back one has to ask a basic question: Is data supposed to be for human consumption or for machine consumption?

For human consumption we have Business Intelligence or BI and dashboards. Lately we also have natural language, and traditionally we have had Google searches that give us data and information. That is data that we can make sense of as humans, and remember, humans have only certain capabilities to read and abstract that data and information.

For machine consumption we have files like CSV, TSV, JSON, etc. These are mostly numerical formats distributed in rows and columns (note that there is also unstructured data not in rows or columns but text that sometimes can be confusing in its representation or absence of narrative). Furthermore, we also have vectors, graphs and logic symbols.

You can see that data for human consumption is closer to information and data for machine consumption is more abstract (arrays of numbers, relationships or logical symbols).

This is more a natural way to see data in our modern world, and technologies like GenAI help to translate those complex vectors into meaningful information that humans can read and interpret.

> When people are still talking about managing data according to their size, they are thinking about how it was twenty years ago. Modern technology pushes us to think about data in a different way. Now, the classes of data for machines and data for humans are very obvious and should be considered in any modern data program.

CHAPTER 4.
The Way We Strategise In Technology And Data

*The essence of strategy is
choosing what not to do.*

Michael E. Porter

The most well-known and influential approaches to strategic thinking have become classics of business analysis. They have filtered down to the general public and pop up in church meetings and environmental activism. The SWOT analysis and Five Forces come from their authors, Clay Christensen and Michael Porter. See [Christensen, 1982] and [Porter, 1985] highlighting the idea of competitive advantage.

Strategists are usually seen as the people who create the plans and apply intellect and sophisticated analytical tools to problems, and are responsible for creating a vision and a mission. However this is only a part of it. According to Michael Porter, strategy is different from aspirations; it is more than a particular action; and it is not the same as a vision or values. Instead strategy defines the organisation's distinctive approach to competing. In other words, strategy is about differentiation to be distinct and to achieve competitive advantage.

Due to new technologies, data strategy, data-led strategy or business-centric data strategy, need a more solid and structured definition that serves as a compass to create that "distinctive approach".

To do that, we need to be knowledgeable of new technologies, and strategists must now be futurists and predict with a degree of confidence the impact of present decisions.

This is because technological developments and advancements are running very fast. For example, from the release of ChatGPT at the end of 2023 until mid 2024, we have had several releases and improvements of all sorts, from image creation to video creation. Speech was rapidly iterated and generative technologies are now incredibly sophisticated.

So what is the best data strategy and technology-led strategy? The answer is an "emergent strategy with a twist". Strategists should now be both the planner and the implementer as proposed by [Powel, 2017]. He offers a beautiful analogy between playing games and climbing mountains:

Due to the vast amount of specialisation, modern technology is similar to playing the ancient Chinese game of Go. This game is particularly difficult. Professional players like Lee Sedol or Lee Chang-ho have the extraordinary ability to spot patterns and identify future moves, and their potential risk and return takes into account the opponent's moves at the same time.

Choosing to play a piece is extremely complex as there are a huge number of possible moves to choose from.

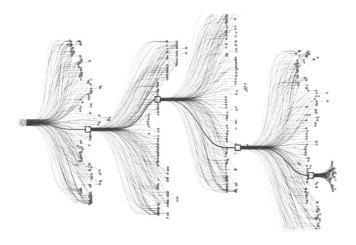

Image source: [Mok, 2016]

Analyzing all those possible lines is key to winning the game. However, the execution is trivial. It is just picking up a piece with your hand and putting it on the board. That is it! Strategy versus Execution.

In the same way, the number of products and services, and the possible combinations of them, is huge! The number of different possibilities to implement data programs and new technologies is so vast nowadays that we need to evaluate the state of a company or of a business like the state of a board of Go. The possibilities must be analysed by an expert, and that is why we need people with experience who have actually done hands-on work using the tools rather than just reading about them on Google. It's the difference between endlessly playing the game of Go versus reading a Wikipedia entry about it.

Shallow knowledge is not enough. The Go master *dan* 9 is similar to an experienced data and technology expert practitioner who can advise and make sound decisions on technology and its next moves. When technology is very expensive, this is key advice.

To sum up, strategists need to be flexible enough to adapt to changes and other players in the market, but rigid enough to deliver value from their decisions.

On the other hand, there are explorers climbing mountains. To climb Everest we know that there are only two routes that offer the best probabilities of success: a) the Southeast Ridge from Nepal and b) the North Ridge from Tibet. That's it! So possibilities are limited and no further pondering is needed.

The real strategy becomes execution: critical choices involving gathering and managing the right team, coping with weather conditions, allocating sherpas, deciding when and where to camp on the way, etc. In the end as put by [Powel, 2017] choosing the right path is not crucial, but taking the right action is.

In the same way, organisations dealing with technology programs need an expert practitioner to organise how many people are in which teams, to choose when to deploy models, to design enterprise architecture, to troubleshoot when algorithms do not work, etc. In other words, an execution strategy.

The new data strategy and data-led strategy must be a hybrid one. Depending on the case, it can be an 80-20 or a 60-40 or a 50-50 planning strategy and execution strategy.

But how to do this when there is an ever-changing landscape of technologies that affect our plans and executions?

The way we should approach strategy and strategic thinking involving technology should be aligned with the work of Henry Mintzberg [Mintzberg, 1985], who proposed the emergent strategy model[2].

This model states that plans change in parallel with discovery. As we learn new things, our plans change alongside our execution.

Emergent strategy must be done by expert practitioners with vast experience to establish flexible plans to cope with new technological developments, but at the same time rigid enough to accomplish goals in the short term. We need to plan ahead foreseeing the vast amount of technical possibilities and be able at the same time to execute them efficiently, or, in our analogy, play Go and climb mountains at the same time.

---

2   To put it in more formal terms, this approach is a combination of the Positioning and Cognitive schools of strategy.

CHAPTER 5.
The Way We Relate With Machines

*Machines take me by surprise
with great frequency.*

Alan Turing

Traditionally, AI was focused on the man-machine relationship and its applications, and even topics like responsible or ethical AI were condensed into the technical dimension, i.e. the man-machine relationship as exposed by Norbert Wiener in his seminal book from the 1940s, see [Wiener, 1965]. Today, AI has more components than the pure machine, for example, social identities, a wide variety of uses, and all personalities of humans applying AI to their daily lives. In business, quality assurance is disappearing as part of the industrial process and becoming more a part of the product itself, and this is a huge difference compared to the traditional view (you can see more dimensions than the classic dichotomy of man-machine).

Think for a moment about our relationships with machines. For example, there is a big difference when we interact with our car or an elevator as we are inside the machine, than with a packing machine in an assembly line in a factory.

The way we treat the machine can be radically different if we are inside or outside the machine. Even unconscious reactions like swearing at the machine when it breaks down alter depending on whether the machine is far or outside our personal space as opposed to how we treat our cars with "love and care", because we are inside the machine. Not only is the machine in our space but we are in the machine's space. Even unconsciously we use phrases like "I need gas" when we mean "The car needs gas": We are one-with-the-machine.

In our modern world, we are one-with-the-machines and I believe that machines and technology will be more integrated to our lives and physical persons in the future.

When we track our biometrics with a smart watch, the machine (the watch) is in physical contact with us all the time. The same is true when we put earbuds in our ears (almost literally inside our bodies). And our phones are an extension of us. We communicate with machines more than we communicate with humans, for example our home assistants like Siri, Alexa and Google Home.

In this sense we are becoming the very definition of cyborgs.

In our modern world, evaluating human performance and mental workload will not be isolated but done in combination with machines. The typical human-centered activities will have man-machine interfaces, and with GenAI, they will include some dialogue too.

Even artists will become man-machine systems specialists for creation and design.

And obviously in scientific activities like experimental validation and model evaluation, a major component will be man-machine systems.

Think for a moment what your relationship is with all machines around you, how you treat them and how you conflate them. We are closer and closer to these machines.

A permanent appendage to us, like our cell phones, makes us cyborgs – part human and part machine. In that way, technology is affecting our relationship with objects.

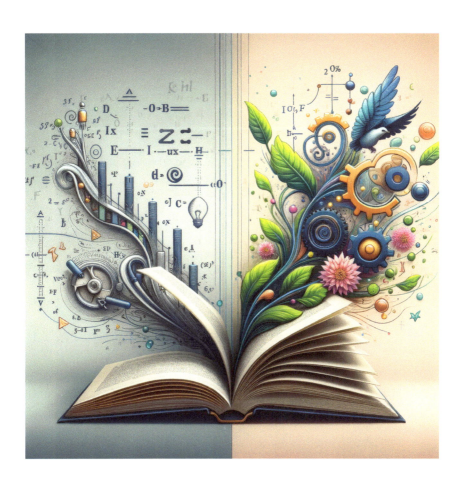

CHAPTER 6.
From Textbook To The New Reality

Entertainment has nothing to do with reality.
Entertainment is antithetical to reality.

Michael Crichton

Real data science is far … very very very far from textbooks. To touch base with reality we need to practice, although some technologies like Google move us away from the practice. I remember seeing this funny cartoon by Barbara Smaller (regular cartoonist at the New Yorker Magazine), depicting a couple in the kitchen where the husband is clearly making a mess and the caption read, *Do you know what you're doing or do you Google-search know?* see [Smaller, A Wife Speaks To Her Husband].

Many courses teach that data science is about developing algorithms and creating mathematical models to represent reality with the objective of a) to optimise it or b) to reflect it, mainly to get valuable insights only visible to the trained, or I would say "initiated", as this area is often perceived as esoteric and unintelligible most of the time.

The models we learn in technical courses, including degree courses in mathematics and physics, have linked the notion of needing perfection to solve cases, and it is even presented as an aesthetic, where the use of a theory or concept is elegantly developed and beautifully applied to cases.

Examples of this are statistical models in basically all textbooks, where we learn how to perform a statistical test to ensure with a certain degree of confidence that something happened or will happen. And even when we acknowledge that the examples have the objective of making the students learn the successful application of a technique, we dismiss the part where the examples are just not part of reality.

The 6-sigma methodology is based on a big assumption: Normality. All data has to follow a normal distribution see [George, 2005], and we know that many cases just do not behave in a normal way. By "normal way" we mean the Gaussian distribution often known as the bell-shaped distribution (the Bell Curve) where the majority of data is concentrated at the center.

Reality points in a different direction where we have to apply semantics and even further interpretations to make sense of data. For example, the first thing many businesses do is make a construct of the actual meaning of data. Or when data is very limited, traditional statistical concepts do not apply; to solve these cases there is no other option but direct experience on the ground.

Traditionally, some senior business leaders found themselves asking for the impossible because they were too far from reality, possibly based on some blog or a Google search, finding themselves and their data science teams in an organisational cul-de-sac. Communication between these leaders and people on the ground was sometimes non-existent because of the different languages they spoke.

But now, with new technologies like GenAI, these leaders are able to be on the ground with their teams and even generate computer code out of natural language.

This however is not that simple, at least not in the short term, as this requires a change in culture and stopping the inertia of the past. They need to understand what the outcome of the tool is and for that, technical teams are still needed. One sure thing is that the communication between technical teams and leaders will change into a more insightful technical one.

On the data science side, new technologies will allow the solving of real world problems, and not only the performance of academic exercises. In the same way as the communication between business leaders and technical team will change, the way to solve real-life problems will change, and the need for understanding the underlying models will be of the utmost importance.

Data science now draws on the classical methodology of empirical research, and its practitioners will likely come from a mathematics or physical sciences background. What this means in practice is expertise in analysis, statistics or modeling, but not necessarily in the practicalities of deploying their models at scale in production. So the reality check will be that these practitioners with their extraordinary academic credentials will need to have proper experience in the field to access senior positions, i.e. getting away from textbooks and applying solutions in real life.

The interface between the senior business leaders and the leaders within the technology teams, including data science teams, is crucial and if both parties adhere to the can-do practical way of thinking, then success will follow. Mathematical understanding of models will be necessary as new technologies can write code easily, and the application of techniques will be more real and applicable than theoretical.

CHAPTER 7.
The Way We See Science

Half of science is asking the right questions.

Francis Bacon

Embedded in modern technology is an ethical problem. We struggle to see it because we have absorbed our school teachings about what science is. Too many of us think that the scientific method, proposed mainly by the philosophical movement in the 17th century, is observed (or otherwise sensed) results from experiments on the assumption that our minds are empty tanks waiting to be filled with information, which we then process to derive a conclusion. Thinking that science is done as observation, hypothesis, experimentation and conclusions is not relevant anymore. Not even in physics, medicine, or any science.

We've moved on since then. The way we do it now is through computational solutions based on mathematical models. Please ask any person who deals with data how they do it to confirm this.

They input the data into the model, see what results and conclusions the model gives and then work backwards to see why it did so, and validate. So the observation comes at the end of the process not at the beginning!

Our ethical programs should consider this new scientific method and how data scientists and other technical staff operate on a day-to-day basis. Moreover, with tools like GenAI, we need to be aware of what is behind the models as it is all no-code or low-code. Hence the traditional scientific method based on empirical philosophy simply does not apply.

So having a tick-box exercise of observations and hypotheses as in the traditional way is not going to solve the problem, precisely because the way we do science now is totally different from what we learnt in school. Instead it is driven by our technological ability, as sustained by Gilbert Simondon, see [Simondon, 2017].

If technical knowledge precedes ethical perception then only a critical design of the technical development will make the difference in both responsible AI and the actual model execution. And this is why we need to change the way we see science and adjust it to modern times, for example the well-known cases of gender and race in recent years.

The main problem lies in the fact that one needs to have a thorough understanding of technology and how it works, and its relationship with science and the techniques behind it, these concepts are certainty not universal but work under the principle of locality and that is why they are sometimes difficult to grasp.

So let us have a quick reflection on science, technique and technology, which are very different and yet are used interchangeably as, for many people, these are interchangeable terms.

Let's take a step back: for example if we have an ethical problem with AI, how do you tackle it? Do you modify the science? Or restrict access to technology? Is it more the techniques used? Where does the problem come from?

As a first approach I would like to define the term technique as used by Feyerabend [Feyerabend, 1976] meaning the use of tools, that is, the real adaptation to the real world comes from techniques but the application of the technique is done somewhere else.

The use of a hoe to prepare the field for sowing is a technique and the person who develops and masters the handling of the tool is a technician. But this is too simplistic an understanding for the complexity of modernity. So I propose the following:

Modern times urge for a division of three related components:

1) science is the method, the abstract concepts behind the techniques

2) techniques are the application of science into problems with generalized applications

3) technologies are the specific application of the techniques to solve particular problems

Without techniques there is no technology and without science there is no technique. The following table gives us a couple of examples:

Science	Technique	Technology
Statistics/ Mathematical theories	Neural network/ Clustering algorithms	AI-Processed Customer Segmentation System
Thermodynamics	Combustion Engine	The Car
Agriculture	Sowing and Weeding	The Hoe

In the same way, in data we have technicians who are very good at coding and pulling resources like machine learning libraries, but in no way are they scientists or technologists as in the definition above.

Technology comes when we get into the application of the technique and develop better tools based on it. The play between technology and technique is always cyclic. A deeper understanding of science is the means by which the techniques develop.

Science is the most abstract of all the three terms. An example of pure science progress is "from theorem 21 to theorem 22" or "from classical mechanics to quantum mechanics"; in the data world, science is the mathematical concept behind the python code and other engineering developments.

The true technologist is someone who understands what is behind the techniques and tools being used and so is able to develop them in adequate applications.

For example, a technological advancement worth mentioning is GenAI. This tool puts into perspective the classical work and approach to technology. Technology in the 21st century is mainly led by data.

Science	Technique	Technology
Data Science	Data Processing	GenAI

Any industry or research field builds on foundations of data. A good example is medicine: in the Middle Ages, this field of study was more of a technique than anything else; in the Renaissance when the field started to actually draw the human body and classify diseases and remedies, the field began to create a strong methodology of analysis and empiricism; in time the medical sciences were able to turn into technology, i.e. the explanation of diseases and remedies including surgeries. In such a way, technique became technology and science, which improved technique. And so on.

It was not until later in the 20th century and mainly in the 21st century that statistical methods and the collection of data became a main pillar in the development of medicine. Even the technological advancements in medicine rely on data for their development, making it both scientific and technological.

Data is a major component in modern science and technology and indeed, to manipulate data we need techniques and technicians. The development of the data-related methods and algorithms come from scientists, both, social scientists and the so-called "hard scientists". Following this process, technology is about making the manual more manual so we can avoid the manual.

Data in the modern world makes humans technical because we modify our environment with it. We do not adapt to our circumstance but we change it. That is the nature of modern humans or I would say technical/technological humans. Animals adapt to changes in their natural habitat, humans do not adapt, they change their surroundings through technology (see chapter 24: "Do People Change Or Is It Just Technology?").

If you really want to tackle issues like ethics in the context of modern technology, you must first reflect on the processes that led to it. We need a serious reflection on science and the scientific method to change preconceived ideas so we can apply sound solutions to difficult modern technological problems while being careful about our environment — because we do not adapt, we change our circumstance.

CHAPTER 8.
New Technologies And Privacy (Or The Lack Of It)

All human beings have three lives:
public, private, and secret.
Gabriel García Márquez

Data privacy is a major topic in technology. There are hearings in the American Congress with the CEOs of social media platforms talking about data usage and privacy, and we have many conferences to safeguard our personal data and protect our privacy. But why is this important?

A main feature that defines human beings is their private space. Having a private space outlines our personality and defines us as a person in society. When we have privacy we choose also to have secrets. And the balance between what we share and what we keep secret delineates our personality and our environment. In other words, privacy defines our boundaries as individuals.

When a person loses privacy, they lose the boundaries that define them as an individual. When everything is public, then there is no line that borders what is and what is not of a person with respect to the society they live in.

Moreover, being private equates to freedom; the freedom of choice as we decide to share or not to share that personal space. When we share our personal space, be it our thoughts, ideas, feelings or body, we share intimacy. Our best friend is our confidant because we share intimate things with them.

Our lover, wife, boyfriend or girlfriend is special because we share our body with them and that makes them unique; that in turn facilitates the forging of a personal relationship between them. And although I have no stance either pro or against infidelities, I can understand that sharing very private information like feelings or our bodies with other people makes the "special" person lose the fact that made them special and that might hurt; it might hurt more than breaking vows or the public humiliation of adultery, because privacy can be more important in human relationships than other things.

Even when reflecting on the "acto contritio", fully explored by Baruch Spinoza in the 17th century, we know that there is a freedom of confession, which also establishes a relationship with God. In the same way, when we "confess" our intimate thoughts and deeds, we establish relationships with others and with ourselves.

When privacy is broken and when all is public, then everybody stays at the same level of a confidant and at the same level of a total stranger. There is no special someone anymore and there is no moral privacy for the individual.

A crush that I have on someone in the school or office, is not a crush if it is public. It loses its essence when shared with the public. It loses its power and becomes trivial. It transgresses our personal ethics and it is a blatant attack against our modesty and personal space.

Thus, privacy is of the utmost importance in our efforts to define ourselves in relation to strangers and society, and in relation to our friends, family and lovers.

Modern technology and social media platforms attempt to destroy the very fabric of human relationships and individuality by trampling on our privacy.

When we talk to people on any chat platform like WhatsApp or Signal, all conversations should be private unless disclosed on purpose by the person. What we search on the Web should be private unless the person decides to disclose. And yes, there is a discussion on surveillance because of searches for illegal things. But does sacrificing our privacy, which also defines us as humans, justifies that intrusion? That is up to the reader to decide.

Modern technology threatens our privacy and we need to be conscious of it and the consequences, like losing individuality.

Privacy defines us as people and gives us a place in our social environment. Privacy is important and it equates to freedom. Moreover, respecting the privacy of others is a sign of respect to the individuality of others.

CHAPTER 9.
The Way We See Data

Data is like garbage.
You'd better know what you are
going to do with it before you collect it.

Mark Twain

Let us start with the question: what is data? The Latin root of the word *data* is just the plural of *datum* and in general it is an abstraction of reality. Data is not information or knowledge, so please note that there is a difference between "data", "information" and "knowledge" and for more on this see the extensive work by [Segal, 2011].

Datum means "given". In Spanish the word for given is *dado* and in Italian it is even clearer because the word for given is *dato*, which happens to be the word for *datum*. But this "given" is something real. In other words, the undeniable real fact is a *datum*.

In Spanish there is a saying "what is given" or *lo que esta dado* which means an actual fact. Even a six-sided die is called a *dado*, which is the factual result of a probabilistic event. In Italian a *dato* is something given as fact like the expression *dato di fatto* or "a given fact", but *dato* is also *datum* and *dati* is *data*.

So traditionally and from the etymology, data is a reflection of reality, but given our modern technology, this is not the case anymore. Data in our modern world must be seen in a different way.

Data is not a reflection of reality any more. We use data to model abstract situations and in that situation, data becomes an abstract entity, sometimes far from reality.

Datum in our modern world is the atom of abstractions; it is the minimal unit with which we abstract the world so we can make sense of it. Abstractions can be representations or even mental images out of real-life objects, phenomena, or processes. For example, the movement of a planet is translated (or abstracted) into numbers: position and speed. In the same way, an assembly line in a factory is represented by numbers: the speed of the line, number of workers, number of pieces assembled, etc. As a matter of fact, human activity or natural phenomena are not themselves, but rather numerical abstractions, since we use machines to analyse them.

For centuries we have been doing this to explain the universe and as one of the most prominent mathematicians in history, Henri Poincaré, stated, "The universe is not geometric, but we make it geometric to understand it" [Poincare, 2007]. In the same way, we produce and use data to make sense of things in our universe.

We also produce and use data to explain the universe itself. For example, the Earth's single revolution around the sun is translated into 365 days, six hours and nine minutes, except for every fourth year when the extra hours add up to an extra day, and the revolution takes 366 days. Abstractions like this allow us to study the behavior of the universe. Moreover, with similar abstractions we can understand and manage business and complex operations the same as things in our daily life.

With numerical abstractions or *data* in general (*data* can be vectors), it is easy to say things about phenomena in the universe, for example, we can predict where a planet will be several months from now, or how many pieces can be produced in a factory if a worker is off sick. That is why traditionally a *datum* has always been numerical. This remains true even when images are translated into matrices of numbers; we now consider data as also words, images, films, numbers and relationships (like in the case of graphs or networks).

Coming back to the etymology of the word, the plural of datum is data. So data is the aggregation of two or more individual "datum". But data on its own does not generate any knowledge. Information has to be drawn out of data before we can generate knowledge. Examples of information are organised patterns of data, for example data points in time (like a time series), or orbits of planets in a chart.

Out of patterns of data, we generate knowledge. Knowledge is the construction of a narrative out of information.[3] As you can see, there is a logical chain from a discrete piece of information (*datum*) to an entire narrative which constitutes knowledge see [Plata, 2007]. In my experience, it is possible for some people to think that "knowledge management" is something other than a logical chain of data or a layered construction of meaning; these people use the word "knowledge management" to mean entirely different from knowledge.

With technologies like GenAI and neutral networks, data becomes an abstraction of an already abstract process or what I call, a meta-abstraction. To explain how we manipulate and treat data to gain knowledge or generate information is a very abstract process, with a lot of chained abstractions in itself. So in our modern world, data is the reflection of an abstraction and not the reflection of reality.

Data is not any more about reality, but about abstract representations of an abstraction itself.

---

3   My view is post constructivist as I integrate language in the construction.

CHAPTER 10.
The Future Of Small Data

Perfection is no small thing,
but it is made up of small things.

Michelangelo

In chapter 3 "The Way We Classify Data," I talk about big data not being a huge problem any more. But I did not talk about small data, which I think is a problem now, especially with more stringent privacy laws and advanced technologies like neural networks.

So what is small data? My definition is totally functional and referential, but first, let's address the question of what big data is. If you try to investigate what it is you will find that there is no formal definition. Some people in the early 2010s put some terabytes or petabytes as a threshold to define it.

For me, big data is data whose amount cannot be handled by traditional tools. For example, if you were defining it in 2005, big data was not handled by traditional tools like MS Excel or limited processing power and storage. What we considered big data in 2005 is now small or small to medium data. Excel in those days could handle a bit more than 64,000 rows, now it can do more than a million.

So big data depends not on the year it is defined, but on the tools available to handle it.

Now "normal" data is such that it can be managed and insights drawn from it with normal tools in normal activities. For example, individual sales per customer for a retailer that could amount to

100 million events is easily handled by a computer, and calculations over it can be done by programming languages like python, which is generally available and open source.

Another angle to define big, small or normal data depends on two variables:

1) the usage
2) processing time

Normal data is used on a recurrent basis, for example periodic reports for a company, trend analysis, forecasting or drawing insights from datasets, e.g. energy consumption, medical trials, etc.

It is not possible for normal usage to handle big data. For example, if the AI model takes weeks to train or run because the amount of data is so large, then we can say that we are dealing with big data. You can see that this definition is referential to the processing time and tools used.

Training a GenAI model with all the information on the web, well, that would certainly be big data. The storage and processing do not fall into the normal range. So the things that you can do with big data are very special.

Now, let's reflect on small data. For centuries, we have been dealing with small data. The main laws of the universe were discovered with small data: gravitational law, electromagnetism, the movement of planets, even calculations of the equatorial circumference of the earth with astonishing precision was done with two data points (and clever reasoning).

So small data has enormous power. The only trick is to know how to deal with it in order to get useful and meaningful insights and knowledge out of it.

In general we see small data in a lot of cases, for example, the fashion industry has new products (with no history) every season, plus fast fashion means that designs change every two weeks to never repeat any of them again.

So analysis for the fashion industry must be done with small data all the time. Even in financial markets, models like GARCH (widely used to estimate the price of a stock at a given time) has a parameter to dismiss the importance of "old data" as it is not relevant to reflect the conditions of the current market. Bottom line: analysis is done on few data points.

Following from Chapter 3 about data classification, data for human consumption is done only in small quantities. Even if we have thousands of data points of sales of a product, executives making decisions generally make them based on aggregate data of a few points so it is digestible for the human mind.

Some cases when small data might be more powerful than big data:

- Customer Acquisition and Retention. Unless it is ultra-micro-super personalization, the only way to make actionable plans on acquisition and retention is by identifying trends. And trends can be identified with small data.
- Potential Risks Identification. This can be done with small data. In fact, adding data here might have the danger of introducing unnecessary noise.
- Innovate. After analyzing the disruptive innovation theory by Clay Christensen, we can definitely say that innovation can be done based on small data.
- Complex Supplier Networks. How many suppliers would you analyse? And how could they interact with each other? Unless the answer is in the millions of suppliers, this is not applicable to any real situation.

- Cost optimisation. This is a good example, as big data is very costly to process.
- Improve Efficiency. This has been done by six sigma processes with very small data and not by big data analysis.

Small data exists everywhere and it is the most useful of all. This is because we can grasp it easily and we can spot trends with simpler models as good as complex algorithms do.

In fact overall trends are equally done with small or big data. A trend will not change because we add more of the same data to the model.

A common question is what would be the minimum data size to apply to a model (like linear regression) so as to achieve statistical significance. The answer depends on each case, but a rule of thumb tells us that we need at least 10 rows per column see [Vittinghoff, 2007], [Peduzzi, 1996] and [Riley, 2019]. So for 25 columns we required 250 rows. This is called the "one in ten rule"[4]

In fact having complex small data is more useful than big data and in fact, the big data problem is heavily surpassed by modern technological tools and AI models. That is why the future of data is in small quantities, either complex or simple, hence the classification of data for humans and of data for machines.

I have even developed specialised techniques to analyse and deal with small data and get meaningful results without the need of huge amounts of data.

---

4   In statistics, the one in ten rule is a rule of thumb for how many predictor parameters can be estimated from data when doing regression analysis (in particular proportional hazards models in survival analysis and logistic regression) while keeping the risk of overfitting low.

Big data is expensive to manage. GenAI can summarize big data and thereby solve in a practical way many big data problems. Counterintuitively, we need to aggregate big data and transform it into small data to communicate it. Big data does not lead to knowledge. Big data is only for machine consumption, not for human consumption. Small data is manageable and understandable by humans. Small data gets trends and has details too. In our modern world small data is often more useful than big data.

CHAPTER 11.
The Way We Work

*All work and no play
makes Jack a dull boy.*

Stanley Kubrick

Today, one of the most important things for people working in or with tech is their well being. For example, a critical aspect of IT workers is burn out. The typical all-nighter, very common in consultancies in the 1990s, is now out of the question. People in tech must be well rested. Long hours are damaging for creativity. And tired or overworked people are more likely to make errors, which are very costly to repair. In my experience the most creative people are those who don't start writing code immediately but do other things, like walk or procrastinate in some way, but then they perform exponentially better than the rest.

So how can we manage projects and teams to take care of our staff without compromising outputs? How can we manage incredibly talented and creative people? What kind of leadership features need to change to accommodate modern ways of working? What kind of managerial responsibilities should we view differently?

Traditionally in Situational Leadership, we have four types of behavior or style: Delegating, Supporting, Coaching and Directing. This model can be found in any Google search and is widely explained and studied in many companies and organisations. More recently we have ways to lead teams like mentoring, training and coaching and then another iteration, many types of coaching, like [Ibarra, 2019]. But none of these models considers the technological environment or the tech staff personalities or the day-to-day of work.

According to the website, "Data Science Central" [Data Science Central, 2019], there is a specific data-science profile with certain skills and capabilities; other organisations discuss their professional qualifications and knowledge (mainly mathematical), but hardly anyone says anything about the human side of these scientists and how quirky some of these off-chart intelligent people can be.

Addressing concerns at a personality level is a critical factor for tech performance and is even more important than money: intellectual reward.

In my experience, many technology practitioners are into Video Games (like myself), so I will make some comparisons with video games that apply to managing tech teams effectively and develop some simple rules to lead teams efficiently. Reflecting on what games give to people and why it is one of the most profitable and successful industries in the world[5] I found the following four points. In the context of my tech teams:

1. Noobs versus Vets

A "noob" or "newbie" is an inexperienced player and a vet is a very experienced one. Experienced gamers hate to play with noobs. Noobs make basic mistakes and generally hold back the team, delay the adventure or ruin the quest. In the same way, the leader of a data science team should be a vet.

In many organisations they make the mistake of putting someone in charge of science or technology who does not understand data or tech. This is due to the inertia that we have from the last decade of the 20th century when now-senior managers started their careers and who refuse to accept that the world has changed the way it functions.

---

5   According to Nielsen's "SuperData" report, the industry's worth was USD $120 billion in 2019. [Venturebit, 2019]

These managers, never having done the tech work themselves, basically lack communication with and empathy towards the work of their team, in other words, they are noobs. This is very frustrating and I have seen many talented people leaving organisations not because of the job itself, but because of the manager.

New technology allows now for managers to be on the ground, but they need to make an effort and be on the ground working shoulder to shoulder with their teams so they become vets. This is empowering and a sign of true leadership.

2. Level Up

An important thing that video games give is a sense of achievement. There is a clear goal or task that serves as a milestone. Once it is reached, the sense of achievement fires the pleasure points in the brain. We're hard-wired for setting goals, then wanting to achieve them and then getting enormous pleasure from having done so. And that's a crucial piece of information. For example, leveling up from level 29 to level 30 is just amazing! Leveling up is normally done as a big event with lights and fanfares. Some players cannot even stop playing until they level up.

Therefore, as managers, it is important to break projects into chunks and "level up" the team and individuals. You gain a clear sense of achievement when there is a clear milestone marking the event and therefore more commitment from the team.

Modern technology, like social media platforms and video games themselves, trigger the need for reward, sometimes immediate reward, and just to keep with the trend and dopamine shots that these technologies give, we must adjust our ways of working and consider this factor as a major feature (see chapter 21 "The Way We See Marketing").

3. Play Your Character

A very important thing video games give is a world (or situation) in which we are the main character; we are the protagonist of the story and everything revolves around us. This sense of ownership is also crucial. When I manage teams, I always make sure that everybody plays a role in the team and even the most junior member has an important task without which the entire project might fail – and they know it. So in a way, they are protagonists of the story, or at least of that level.

Sometimes, especially in big corporations, people feel that they are just a small cog in the massive engine of the organisation and if they do or they don't… well, it doesn't matter.

So to keep the team motivated, you have to address individual ownership. I am not saying this is easy, this can be difficult as you also have to manage cross-functional and knowledge-management responsibilities. But we as managers should nurture teams with a high self-esteem.

4. Save the game!

Finally, a thing that video games give to players is a safety net. Before fighting the "big boss" one can save the game and if one fails, well… just go back to where you saved the game and try again.

A safety net is very important in data and tech teams; and this is a managerial duty! You have to provide the correct environment for the team to be brave and try new things, knowing that if they fail they can try again. If there is a dire consequence for failing, everybody will be afraid to try anything; and innovation in the team will die.

This point is of the utmost importance as the essence of tech's success lies in innovation and letting teams try new things.

This is 100% the manager's responsibility as they have the global view of projects and connections with other initiatives in the organisation, so they can build the optimal safety net in case anyone falls.

Saving the game takes time, so knowing when to "save" the game and let people adventure themselves – which means occasionally running on thin ice – is an art. But that is exactly why we need experienced managers to run these teams.

Silicon Valley's mantra of "fail fast, fail often" has to change to simply "fail less", which means failing with little consequence due to "saving the game" strategically.

> *Treat your tech teams and staff with the lessons learnt from video games, stimulate them intellectually. But also give them a sense of achievement, ownership and a safety net to be brave and try courageous things and innovate. It is a management duty and responsibility to do this.*

CHAPTER 12.
The Way We See Functional Stupidity

*Never ascribe to malice that which
is adequately explained by stupidity.*

Napoleon Bonaparte

The term "functional stupidity", coined by scholar Mats Alveson, has defined many functions in a vast range of organisations. As stated in his [Alveson, 2012], there is a need for "functional stupids" in organisations to keep things moving[6].

These kinds of profiles are better suited for operational roles, rather than strategic or intellectual roles. For example, data science, analytics and in general technology are at their core, intellectual endeavors. However there are people, sometimes at a high level, in charge of the company's data and technology functions who act like functional stupids, blocking any communicative action as per Jurgen Habermas in his [Habermas, 1984] (see chapter 16 "Applied Philosophy In The Age Of GenAI"). This thwarts any progress. This might be due to the lack of practical experience or knowledge.

But how does it happen that someone without practical know-how achieved such a position of dominance? Once again, there is an inertial momentum in the ways of working and organising companies and projects. It comes from the last decades of the 20th century as shown by [Isenberg, 1986], where problems within organisations were solved by comparing the thinking-aloud protocols when managers were pursuing their business

---

6   It is not my intention to be pejorative, I am only using the same terminology and concept as Alveson.

careers, as if they were still in school solving a business case in class.

Starting in the 1990s we can see two visions for solving problems: first, the theoretical in which we have a problem well-defined, normally formulated by others, and with all information required for the solution. In addition, we normally used to have one correct answer and had one or several methods to get the correct answer. Obviously because of the problem being theoretical, the answer often was not related to reality (see [Neisser 1976], and [Wagner & Sternberg 1985]) and also my notes on the chapter about "textbooks and reality" in this same book.

In contrast, we had the second way of solving problems, a practical approach which involved everyday-life issues, which commonly were ill-defined and missing information essential to solution. These problems had multiple solutions, each associated with liabilities and assets. Solving them required multiple methods to obtain each solution and most importantly, all related to day-to-day experiences [Wagner, 2002].

What we need to do is to enhance both of these methods, the theoretical and the practical, to take into account the advancements in AI and computing, and the wider applications of advanced mathematical modeling. Although there are many problem-solving techniques, I classify them into two groups:

1) mathematical techniques, which include:
   a) prove and disprove being the most common, proving that the solution does not exist
   b) reduction and disassembling, originated in the solution of linear algebra problems and most commonly known as "divide and conquer"
   c) analogy and abstraction, which is the most common application of mathematical models, in which we have one model applicable to many cases.

2) the six-sigma techniques, which include:
   a) root cause analysis (RCA)
   b) hypothesis testing
   c) trial and error, which is also part of continuous improve-
      ment.[7]

One of the main issues that affect AI and its management is the fact that some people who started their careers in the 1990s are now at executive levels and still apply all the things they learnt about the methods from those days. Now, when they try to ex-trapolate those ideas and ways of thinking into the modern world, it just does not work unless they know how to combine the above problem-solving techniques.

Sometimes, when observing this, some managers get into a functional stupidity framework, in which the motto is: "This has to work". And then they force results into their tech teams.

Some managers in charge of data functions made decisions that did not make any sense, for example, buying outdated tech-nologies, or implementing Business Intelligence (BI) solutions when what they really wanted was machine-learning develop-ments or implementing expensive platforms to productionise when what they were really trying to do was to prototype solu-tions.

This is clear when executives in charge of data functions and AI developments, sometimes with absolutely no experience in data or analytics or even a brief understanding of mathematics with totally unrelated academic backgrounds or sometimes none, ask for the impossible in a limited amount of time.

----

7   Within all these techniques there are many methods. For example inside RCA we have Ishikawa diagrams, 5 whys, Pareto analysis, fault and success trees, and why-because analysis and like this example with all the others. But given the nature of their approach I can say that there are only two groups.

Of course there are people in high level roles who, not having worked directly with data, nonetheless have a thorough understanding of technology and science. But this comes with a huge extra effort to catch up with the latest models with people on the ground to understand their position and roles.

Following that inertial momentum, the relationship between managers and analysts was that the manager asked for some information, chart or "insight" from the analyst, without even knowing how to get it or really understanding the request or the outputs. They seemed to live in a movie where all the answers were scripted in advance to show them in meetings and fill their presentations.

In the last decade of the 20th century, data was limited and its analysis was mainly to back up managerial decisions. Actuaries and financial mathematicians were of the utmost importance as the financial planning and understanding of projections were one of the main problems to solve.

However, by the second decade of the 21st century, almost all functions are data-led: customer relations, marketing, merchandising, supply, logistics. Even finance relies immensely on analytics and advanced modeling. A deep understanding of data, and of handling and managing huge amounts of it, was key to the development of the functions.

Today, as they are normally out of their depth (as they have never worked on data closely before), managers in charge of data programmes normally depend entirely on their subordinates (sometimes the most junior of them) to make decisions on data organisation, resourcing, platforms and programmes. And then they make executive decisions based on the regurgitated basic understanding of the partial views of sometimes junior members of staff, some google searches and some amateur opinions on blog posts.

It has taken until now for tech areas to acquire the maturity that other areas like marketing have (and marketing has been with us for more than half a century, while data science only for some years). Therefore, the idea of an analyst being part of the executive board taking technical decisions instead of business decisions was unthinkable for the traditional managers (which in this case act like functional stupids). Fortunately, this is now changing. Versed tech experts are becoming more strategic and therefore have greater latitude to make meaningful decisions at a C-level in business.

Technology as magic.

Due to the poor understanding of data, models and mathematics in some management layers, people can get away with "talking smoothly" to managers, and even promising the impossible.

In these cases, data is like magic: no one knows how it works and it creates the illusion of something out of nothing. The limited knowledge and understanding is food for many to take advantage of.

Even with new technologies like GenAI we still need data experts at an executive level who

1) Understand the science behind the new techniques
2) Understand data and how to optimise its monetization
3) Have some experience troubleshooting in specific technological cases, which implies understanding problem-solving techniques.

Finally, the concept of a "citizen data scientist", popularized in the mid 2010s is frankly insulting. It was designed by people who do not have any appreciation of data, or have an understanding of science or technology, and do not consider the subtleties of the practice while trivialising the serious work of technical people. This will change in the future due to specialisation and the introduction of low-code technologies.

In data and technology we cannot have functional stupids. Functional stupids are good at the operational functions. But technical and scientific work is mostly intellectual where we need communicative action to boost progress and innovation. Functional stupidity could disappear within technology, and problems will be ill-proposed, with imperfect data and short time to solve. Therefore, approximations and partial results should be published openly in order to allow development.

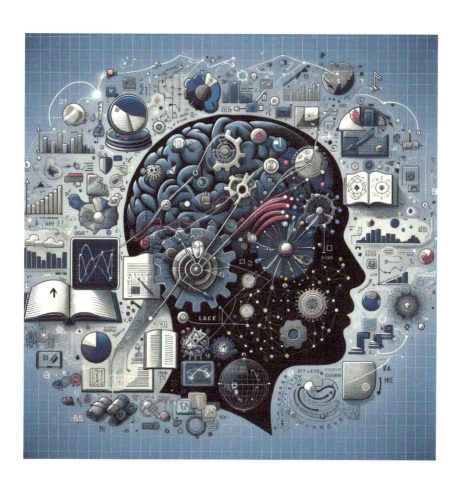

CHAPTER 13.
The Way We Learn

*The only education worth
anything is self-education.*

Isaac Asimov

Traditionally, the norm was to learn from books which have a structure (well, most of them). We started learning from the simplest and moved to the hardest, or in chronological order or even in a more pedagogical way with theory and examples combined.

But technological change is moving too quickly for the more static publishing industry. Instead, information is found on Reddit or other platforms. This forces us to avoid consulting books, let alone reading them from cover to cover or learning from them. And that is one of the reasons why I decided on the format of this book: to facilitate the construction of a map.

In the absence of books and the rise of technological tools like Google or GenAI, we get flashes of information that we need to build ourselves. That is what I call a "cognitive map". We form cognitive geographies in our head, and connect concepts and ideas based on the information we get.

Let's say that we want to know about the theory of relativity. The first thing we do is to Google search it. The first hit from the search is Wikipedia, which is both very thorough and very confusing. It is certainly not for learning what the theory is about. It has formulas that for most are unintelligible and jumps from topic to topic with a number of links to other keywords, which take us to other pages which are equally confusing.

So we abandon that and go to the next hit, which is a similar page but more technical, in fact it is too advanced for the general reader. The next hit is more about the history of relativity, which starts around a century before Einstein published his paper at the beginning of the 20th century. And so on with other hits. Information on the web is not curated by a librarian or a specialist, but presented to us by an algorithm that we know nothing about.

To build our knowledge based on flashes of "unstructured" information, not chronological or not pedagogical, we are forced to build a jigsaw puzzle for which neither we know the image of the puzzle nor the number of pieces. So, the easiest way to build knowledge is through a map which, in the end, is what we actually do.

With GenAI, we have a similar situation, possibly less chaotic than a Google search, but nevertheless iterable. We can iterate, as in a conversation, to get more information. Having tried this, I ended up having a very similar case as the previous one and still had to build a cognitive map.

Learning from the web or from unstructured information means that we need to over-impose a certain narrative (or cognitive map) to what we get as input.

ChatGPT gives us summaries, so people do not read books. They do not even read the summary of the books but the bullet points of the summary of the book that might not based on an actual input of the book, but rather on the opinions and reviews of other people that are publicly available on the web.

Therefore, schools should focus more on critical thinking, and teaching students how to easily and quickly fill in the epistemological gaps of the overwhelming wave of information we get everyday, and how bridges of knowledge can be built.

Moreover, we cannot ask students to write as in the old days when we learnt from books[8], subconsciously copying the format of what we read. (see chapter 22 "The Way We Write"). Education should focus on building cultural atlases in which each cognitive map is unique for each individual and adjust quickly to new available technology.

The modern situation becomes clear when we accept the fact that we no longer learn from books. When we have flashes of scattered information everywhere, we need a different learning and teaching method. Modernisation in schools is a must in order to adapt to GenAI and other technologies and change the classic structures.

In the end, there might be a new epistemological theory on how to learn. We will not learn chronologically, or "in order". The structure of knowledge and how it is presented to us, and even the argumentation will be different if we cannot replicate that structure. In my opinion, we are in need of cognitive maps, epistemological geographies and knowledge atlases[9].

Education should be about formation and not information. Education is no longer about facilitating information acquisition but is instead about managing that information in a way that makes sense. We need to teach students to create cognitive maps, knowledge atlases and epistemological geographies so we can grasp information and apply it to our modern technological world.

---

8   Books have structure and our educational system taught us to follow an order of knowledge: introduction, development and conclusion. Even when writing an essay we are recommended to follow that same structure.
9   As a note aside, I have a theory for teaching technical subjects that I think is more appropriate. I call it the trochoidal model for learning science, in which activities and theory move in three axes following a trochoid or a loxodrome.

CHAPTER 14.
Technology And Memory

The pure present is an ungraspable
advance of the past devouring the future.
In truth, all sensation is already memory.

Henri Bergson

In English there is a phrase that refers to the action of memorising. It is "learning by heart". It is interesting that the phrase refers to knowing something. But where does that knowledge sit?

Learning by Heart

Learning by heart was the dominant method of learning in the 19th century. Mnemonic rules were taught and still being taught in schools for some subjects. for example, the SUVAT equations in mechanics or the SOH CAH TOA in mathematics for trigonometrics. But remember when the teacher said, "You have to learn the poem by heart by tomorrow," and knowing poems by heart like "tyger tyger burning bright…" before entering university had a biographical notoriety.

Recalling by heart (or by memory) extracts from famous texts or religious books was the token of civil and intellectual education and class in those days. In countries like Mexico this was the norm; in fact education in the form of erudition was highly regarded until the end of the 20th century.[10]

With modern technology, learning by heart is certainly a thing of the past. Having all the information we might need in our cell phones waives the need for memory. However I can say that my

---

10 For more on this see [Steiner , 1991]

personality is shaped by what I learnt by heart. Why? Because when one learns by heart that thing is "in the heart"; one grows with it and that poem that we learnt in middle school for which we had little or no understanding takes significance some years later and when we are thirty years old we say, "Finally I understand what that poem means" This understanding changes because when one hits forty, and then the same happens when one turns fifty.

The poem grows with us through our life and matures with us. It helps us to find solace in difficult times and also to be generous or dignified when we need to.

Why? Because it is in our heart. The heart is where love is, it is where emotions and sentiments live. The things that we learn by heart are there because we love them. And even the minimal stimulus, like a shrimp on a plate or a house painted blue, can trigger dear memories with nostalgia. As Milan Kundera mentioned in one of his books, nostalgia is the essence of memory.

Learning by heart is always accompanied by something else: hate, love or life itself. Learning by memory is only to pass a test and forget about it afterward. Learning by memory is ephemeral and lacks meaning.

Learning by heart is there to stay. When you learn by heart you are prepared to make that a part of you and not just a mere memory.

Learning by memory

Learning by memory is typical of modern technology. The electronically stored and the huge inventory of information has been such as to make mnemonic rules obsolete. There is no longer an agreed set of canonical texts, dates or events that mark certain civility or class. Everything is on the phone, on Google, on our calendars or even on our personal digital assistants that remind us of appointments and things to do during the day. However, just as the daily appointments, everything becomes ephemeral.

The huge exposure to the information avalanche and synchronic immediacies of our social media platforms leaves little time and little mental space for the cultivation of memory. Think: when was the last time you needed to memorise something?

I wonder if our educational system is making younger generations amnesic, which could lead to a deculturalisation of our society, norms and even political systems due to the lack of formational anchors.

On a day-to-day level we no longer learn by heart; we learn by memory and our textual memories are shallow. And recalling something is reduced to a bunch of keywords that allow us to electronically search for more information. In other words, we learn by memory like the famous story by Jorge Luis Borges "Funes The Memorious", where Funes has a photographic memory of everything, but with no context. If this trend continues, learning by heart will cease to exist.

Is this good or bad? I am not one to judge.

And one more point on the essence of memory and learning by heart: In his paper [Hepper, 2012] states that nostalgia is a "complex emotion that involves past-oriented cognition and a mixed affective signature. The emotion is often triggered by encountering a familiar smell, sound, or keepsake...". So once again, nostalgia and memory are closely linked.

The question is that with modern technology, affections might be more electronic and ephemeral than life-lasting and internalised. So the next iteration after Kundera and Hepper is that nostalgia will be linked to things that only existed in the electronic repository. And then we will have the worst nostalgia of all, which is yearning for what never happened.

If after reading this you consider important learning by heart, what would you learn by heart or what would you tell students to learn by heart? What would those young people have in their memories to grow with them and accompany them in their lives?

Learning by heart is special because it is with us permanently in latency and only becomes patent when we need it. Playing between latency and patency is the secret of permanent memory in modern times, but this only happens when the memories are in the heart. And in modern times there is no worse nostalgia than to yearn for what never happened.

CHAPTER 15.
The Way We See Information

*Where is the knowledge we
have lost in information?*

T. S. Eliot

I keep hearing things like "that visualisation is too difficult", referring to images like this one:

This image was generated over the TensorFlow Projector,[11] which is an open source and free-to-use visualiser. I used my own data from a public source (kaggle) of 15,000 data points and generated vectors of 256 dimensions each (as you can see from the picture).

---

11 Available at https://projector.tensorflow.org

Then I applied the T-SNE algorithm (from TensorFlow) to visualise clusters. In this way we can start getting insights out of the data.

The question is: How can I put this information in a traditional way so the visualisation is not "too difficult"?

Traditionally, the method used to analyse data and other phenomena in nature was the so called *"ceteris paribus"*,[12] which tested one variable while keeping the others constant. This method was used by epidemiologists, medical researchers and economists, these later ones being the most prominent users of it.

Due to the complexity of human economic activity, analysing several variables at the same time was very difficult and sometimes practically impossible. For example, in the 17th century when we did not even have calculators, the economist William Petty used the method to analyse his labor theory of value. One of the most famous examples is John Stuart Mill and Alfred Marshall in the 19th century using it to analyse partial equilibrium analysis.

When I took my course of mathematical economics in the late 1990s, we still studied with this method, and even methods like differential calculus in several variables was done in this way: one variable at a time assuming the others were constant or not moving.

So the norm to understand data through graphic representations would have looked like this:

---

12 Ceteris Paribus is a Latin phrase, meaning "other things equal"; or "all other things being equal", "other things held constant", "all else unchanged", or "all else being equal".

This is what most of the people expect. This image was created in LibreOffice Calc with arbitrary data.

However, with more advanced technological tools, we have the ability to cross reference a number of variables and analyse them simultaneously. As a result, we generate more complex data and generate multidimensional number arrays to represent phenomena; and all this on a normal commercial laptop for a normal business project.

We also have tools – free and available tobasically anyone – to visualise these data. One of the main needs when handling more complex data and complex analysis, usually done by machines involving several variables at the same time, is to change the way we see data representations which are aimed for humans as opposed to data aimed at machines.

Libraries like D3.js with visualisation like this one are now more common; the following images are standard templates of visualisations in D3.js[13]:

_____

13 Available at https://d3js.org

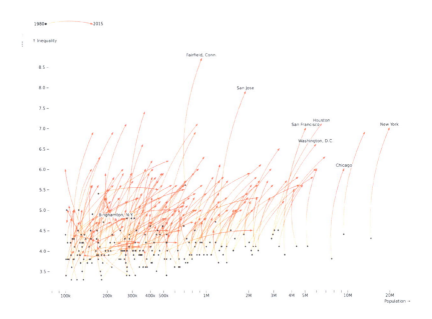

Image taken from D3.js website templates, available at https://observablehq.com/@d3/inequality-in-american-cities?intent=fork accessed on 10/3/24.

Once again, referring to the chapter 3 "The Way We Classify Data", data for human consumption would be graspable. But we need also to change the our paradigm for understanding data, and start seeing these kinds of visualisations as normal.

In the same chart, we can see four or five variables interacting at the same time:

1) amount of sales
2) types of product
3) market and
4) time

We tend to use different colors for products, different sizes of bubbles for amount of sales, in different positions in the chart for markets, and lines joining them to other bubbles that represent their position in the past and their evolution to present. In comparison, using ceteris paribus would require twelve charts instead of just one.

Another example is taking notes. Traditionally taking notes was done in cards or normal documents, where we needed to code titles, events, subjects, etc. with different styles: bold, italics, fonts, bullet points, etc. I remember looking for a topic among all those notes or cards was a complicated task in itself. But if I were to use a new technology like Obsidian.md,[14] which is also free, I could build knowledge graphs out of notes. I even have my notes from books and papers in the form of a knowledge graph which is a lot easier to read and consult. It's a radical change.

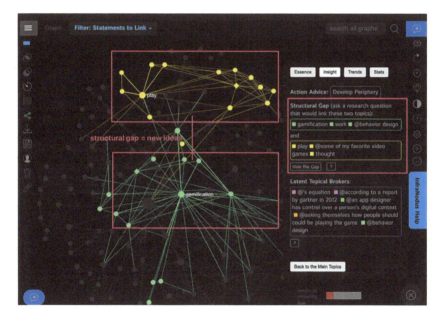

Image taken from obsidian.md forum available at https://forum.obsidian.md/t/how-to-extract-taken-notes-for-writing-new-article/11511 accessed on 10/3/24

This is also a more modern way to visualise and refer to notes using modern technology.

---

14 Available at https://obsidian.md

With modern technologies we need to change the way we see information and get used to making more abstractions out of data. Traditional visualisations are fine and useful, but as we have more tools to analyse complex phenomena, we need to keep up as humans and get used to more complex visualisations

CHAPTER 16.
Applied Philosophy In The Age Of GenAI

Be a free thinker and don't accept
everything you hear as truth.
Be critical and evaluate what you believe in.

Aristotle

This is the most abstract chapter of the book. It is a quick recount from Empiricism to Post Structuralism. Although it sounds like a philosophical theory it is nonetheless applicable to how we see our modern world.

One of the first things they did with ChatGPT was writing essays and assignments, and doing homework for courses in schools. And this is one of the things that will not change. So how can we change the way we see education? And what would be the repercussions of working with ChatGPT to generate essays?

The problem started with marking essays, which was one of the hot topics for AI some years ago. Would one algorithm be able to mark another algorithm? It sounds insane, right? It is not about humans anymore! Algorithms writing essays on behalf of the students, and algorithms marking essays on behalf of the teachers.

The point is that in the absence of humans, we train the models to write and mark essays according to canons, and our canons come from the 1700s. So no real evolution there.

For example, attempts to address a thesis' clarity using a convolutional neural network (CNN) or identifying sentence sequences are based on rules suggested by the Empiricists in the 16th century. Authors like [Ridley, 2020] proposed a Graph Convolutional Network that took into account features like length, readability, complexity, variation and sentiment, and [Zhang, 2019] who proposed a list of four recommendations for students. And ChatGPT would do a similar job.

I have my philosophical reservations on this one. So let me explain:

To a large extent, a technical bibliography concentrates on very tactical problems, many of which have been addressed by GenAI. However, this new technology is still based on the canonical model and there is little reflection on the language theories behind the practical developments of meaning and logic, unless one gets into its proper philosophical turf and tries to understand authors like Paul Ricœur, Gerard Genette, Ludwig Wittgenstein and even Noam Chomsky's early work on pure linguistics.

So let's start our journey with the empiricists, mainly John Locke and David Hume (see [Locke, 2017] and [Hume, 2007]). They argued that a good essay must have a good association of ideas, which are based on three factors:

1) Similarity
2) Contiguity
3) Causality; this last one – in my personal opinion – was taken directly from Aristotle from his book "On Memory" [Aristotle, 1984], what he calls "sequentiality", a term later used by George Berkeley and Thomas Hobbes.

These three factors were considered essential for expressing ideas and writing essays for generations. Not only did the empirical method have an impact on writing, but also on science, giving us what we now know as the scientific method, firstly proposed by Sir Francis Bacon around the mid-1600s. As a result, they are integral to the canon.

Many years later, in the late 19th century, these empirical ideas were taken by the fathers of semiotics, Ferdinand De Saussure and Charles Peirce, who argued that the signification of words and moreover the identification of key words were important to convey messages [De Saussure, 1959] and [Peirce, 1996].

These ideas were developed later by the post structuralists Roland Barthes and Gilles Deleuze, stretching the semiotic argument of isolated words into sentences and their location in the text [Barthes, 1986] and [Deleuze, 1994]. Personally, I like Deleuze's earlier work on hermeneutics and even his doctoral thesis about Bergson fascinated me … but I digress… Up to this point techniques like NLP followed these ideas to decode language into a computer program and GenAI bases its marking based on these premises. So would there be a further development of the essay as a literary genre? The answer seems to be no.

Contemporary to the post structuralists, we also have the pragmatists like Jurgen Habermas, who proposed the idea of communicative action (mentioned in chapter 12 "The Way We See Functional Stupidity") that has at its core the intersubjective argumentation. I personally agree with Habermas and I like his theory and the influence he had on some of my favorite writers like Gunter Grass, Patrick Süskind and even Milan Kundera, see [Habermas, 1984].

Jurgen Habermas argues that comprehensiveness does not ensure explanatory power. And in order to explain something, there is the need for argumentation or "critical explanations", which only happens when there is some intersubjective communication.

So how about, based on his theory of Communicative Action, we build an AI-intersubjective rationality tool that can help the student write a better essay?

The only way I can see a personal and collective intellectual development is by implementing some kind of intersubjective argumentation as the basis to follow our logical journeys, and then to use GenAI tools as a sounding board to write essays.

To better explain these different ideas a diagram can help. In the classical Cartesian frame, we have a subject-object relationship, in which the subject is transitive to the object but not the other way around. This is known as the "Cartesian Duality". For Descartes the subject is a thinking core, discreet and whole in itself. Its object is where the action of the subject falls. An example in the communication area would be an order that is obeyed and not questioned, see [Descartes, 1998].

This changes with Karl Popper in his framework of instrumental, normative and dramaturgical rationality where he proposes a subject-subject communication (or intersubjective) but with an object in between, and although there is some debate, this communication is done through an object, see [Popper, 1992]. An example of this

Traditional Cartesian framework:

The message is uni-directional

Karl Popper framework of instrumental, normative and dramaturgical rationality

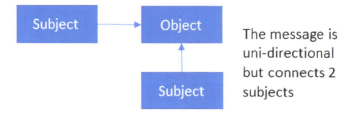

The message is uni-directional but connects 2 subjects

Habermas however proposes a more direct approach: a subject-subject or intersubjective argumentation.

Communicative rationality framework:

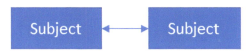

The message is bi-directional
and requires argumentation

This argumentation is normally done by professors in a one-to-one conversation with the students, however with GenAI tools this has gradually diminished. So how about this as a possible solution: GenAI plays the part of the professor and the process could be done in the following way:

Student writes a sentence → Algorithm looks for similar sentences in the known literature →Student gets back related thinking → Student gets an argumentation exercise based on known literature

This epistemological-based proposal brings a number of advantages:

- Students will connect with all relevant bibliography
- Students will have counterpoints and similar arguments from the already known literature
- Literature review will be more focused and faster

- Students will get an AI-sounding board for their ideas, and therefore deeper understanding
- Argumentative-based epistemology will be continuous as it does not need to wait for the tutor/lecturer to interact
- A form of mentor-mentee relationship will be built instead of a mere teacher-pupil
- Increase critical thinking of students
- According to the epistemological theory, this intersubjective exercise will create a better narrative and the further development of the genre

This method can be extended to businesses and decision-making processes in organisations to enhance communicative action and stop functional stupidity, which is inherently a good thing.

The problem of writing an essay in the canonical way has been surpassed by technologies like GenAI. In order to progress pedagogically and philosophically as well as literarily, we need the human input hand-in-hand with the machine. The machine should be playing a key part in the intersubjective dialogue in order to create meaningful new ideas, critical thinking and literary proposals. The benefits for students and organisations are many: enable communicative action at all levels.

CHAPTER 17.
The Way We Connect Knowledge And Leadership

Management is doing things right; leadership is doing the right things.

Peter Drucker

In modern technology programs, the level of specialisation is so high that it is practically impossible to organise a structured team and develop projects without first having a strategy. Sometimes DevOps engineers are specialised in only one tool. Generalists are also necessary.

Traditionally businesses deploy teams in an empirical way. We see that we need someone to perform a task. Then we hire that person. And finally we allocate that person under a given structure without thinking what the correct or more optimal layout should be. For example, very technical people doing high-profile computer programming like coding, then reporting to the marketing manager. Or a project manager reporting to a database administrator.

What we need in order to integrate teams with a wide range of specialisations and knowledge is a more modern view of leadership.

In fact, when we talk about knowledge management, we should be talking about the way we set teams and deploy them in projects. People normally mix and confuse terms and talk about knowledge management when what they really mean is data management or information systems' governance. That is why it is important to know the difference between data and knowledge (see chapter 9 "The Way We See Data").

On some occasions, tech-related projects have an innovation component, for example, a process design project or a new marketing campaign. Managers employ highly capable individuals or hire top talent but then often set them to work within structure and processes that doom them to failure. This is mainly because of lack of consistency between the business model[15] and the way teams are deployed in a project context.

These projects can range from being cutting edge (or at least bleeding edge) or being new to the company to normal operational maintenance, and even when technology makes things "easier", the way in which we deploy teams should be carefully thought through to succeed.

In classic strategy theory, there are four main ways to organise teams to successfully land different kinds of tech projects. This diagram was developed by [Clark, 1992], [Christensen, 200] and [Patanakul, 2012], see diagram below:

Image taken from [Christensen, 2000]

---

15 I am using the Johnson-Christensen business model definition, see [Johnson, 2008]

Dotted lines = communication lines
Solid lines = reporting lines
VP = Vice President in charge of the area

Depending on the type of development or project teams can be

a) functional
b) lightweight
c) heavyweight
d) autonomous

Of course there are variations, but these formats are a good guideline to start a project.

There are two main factors to take into consideration while deploying teams: The type of project and the interdependencies within the business processes.

For example, while working on high technology novelty or radical innovation like applied R&D, the best way is to set an autonomous team, while in continuous improvement initiatives, a lightweight team would suffice.

The following table illustrate this point:

Team	Type of Project	Interdependency	Implementation Manager
Functional	BAU, or refine existing operating model	Strong interdependencies	Junior
Lightweight	Improving existing process	Predictable interdependencies	Junior to Mid-to-senior
Heavyweight	Create a new process	Unpredictable interdependencies arise but not often	Mid-to-senior to Senior
Autonomous	Create a new business model	Unpredictable interdependencies are often present	Senior

Table taken from [Plata, Ioannou, 2024]

Because of advancements in technology and the high degree of specialisation and expertise, the size of the team plays a small role in the actual setting and the most important thing is to choose the correct manager level and the actual structure of the team.

Project managers, scrum masters, product managers, product owners and other related execution managers should evolve into a holistic implementation manager. This implementation manager should perform the strategy for the new ways of working in a modern tech environment.

Skills specialisation will force us to have hybrid teams layouts. For example, a combination of heavyweight with autonomous, or any other combination of the classic four types.

A good option to deal with new technologies and executing them through projects and products is the LIGHT methodology, which lays down organisational strategies for project implementation; this was proposed in conjunction with Jovana Ioannou in [Plata, Ioannou, 2024] even proposing the creation of an "implementation manager" overarching projects and products roles while developing strategy at the same time.

The most important thing in modern technology projects is to keep knowledge and communication flowing. This can only be done through the correct team setting and holistic implementation management. However, due to technical specialisations, we will need to take a close look at how we can appropriately combine the classic four types and make efficient hybrid teams to implement developments successfully.

CHAPTER 18.
Look Who's Talking Now

*The eagerness of a listener quickens
the tongue of a narrator.*

Charlotte Bronte

One of my reflections with new technological developments is the recognition of the narrative identity. In literature, it is important that the reader recognise who is talking. We call that the narrative identity. In complex books, it is possible to have a range of ways to tell a story. Sometimes, the author is talking in the first person or the author has a character of the novel talking or a third person narrates the story. There can be many options and combinations, and in literature there are any number of examples.[16]

We have the same situation in science: who is actually saying things? Is it the original researcher or is he just repeating someone else's theory or conclusions? Is what we learn in schools not the teacher's knowledge or the textbook author's knowledge, but the teacher's interpretation of the textbook, written by someone who in turn interpreted something from the original researcher? And that is why I always recommend going to the original sources all the time whenever possible. Not only should we read secondary sources, but the originals too.[17]

While it can be occasionally convoluted and difficult to identify this narrative identity in science, it is always possible to do it. The way concepts and ideas are presented to us depend on

---

16 For more on this see [Canaparo, 2000]
17 For more on this see [Plata, 2005]

this narrative identity. We can say, "Yes of course, this author is a defender of this or the other idea, that is why he says these things the way the author says it".

With new technologies however, especially with GenAI, we really don't know who is talking! Is it the algorithm? And if the algorithm is saying something in a certain way or empathising some ideas on some delicate topic, who can we go to? How can we discuss this? Is it that the algorithm is from the political left or right? Is the algorithm neutral? Which begs the question: is there such a thing as neutral speech?

The only way to identify who is talking is by increasing our critical thinking and questioning the information in front of us. If we lack this critical thinking then the trend will be to accept what the algorithm is telling us as truth, and the generalised acceptance of it at face value will only standardise our opinions. If we do not exercise this literary analysis, in the future there will be no opinion except the algorithm's.

Once again, critical thinking is key to deal with new technologies and realize who the narrative identity is and how to improve consciously our consumption of information from these technologies.

Chapter 19.
The Way We See New Skills

*It's fun making new skills
for new characters.*

Masahiro Sakurai

New technologies and advances in areas like GenAI have affected all data scientists. Ironically, we are now in less need of them and more in need of people with critical thinking skills. Data engineers are needed as long as they are proficient in managing data, the same with people who can run data pipelines and machine-learning algorithms in production.

So when we are in the position to interview a data scientist or a technical person, what should we look for today? We used to say that when recruiting, we were in search of a "unicorn", that is, a person that simply did not exist, a person with the technical knowledge and experience in all domains at the highest level. But now due to specialisation and technologies, we need to step back and think about what kind of skills we will need.

Traditionally, people used to be proficient using the sliding rule or using logarithms tables, but technology has actually made them obsolete. I think that very few people of younger generations even bother to know how to multiply with logarithms. And why would they? Since the 1980s we have had calculators that could do that. And since smart phones, we have had technology on our mobile phones to calculate logarithms. So technology has also changed the way people need and look for skills in people.

The amount of information available on the web also moved memory into a second place (see the chapter 14 "Technology

And Memory"). Why would I memorise the formula to solve second-degree equations if it is available at the tip of my fingers on a cell phone?

Because of new technologies, the most important thing is to understand concepts and be able to apply them in practical cases. One of the skills that would be useful is to understand artificial intelligence models so we know how they work, how we can improve and how we can modify them to apply them in specific cases.

Some time ago I would have said creative skills were the future because machines were not able to be creative, but with GenAI developments, I think almost all the creative jobs can be done by just asking for them. Skills from photographers, designers and copy writers, along with data scientists and computer scientists, are unfortunately less needed now with new technologies.

It is of absolutely no use to ask people things that can be known or done with a simple Google search. With GenAI at anyone's reach, generating code in any programming language is simple. Live-coding interviews should be a thing of the past because we normally Google errors and import libraries, and once again, with GenAI, we basically can have the skeleton of any code. And to test someone's memory might be an indicator of being more in the past than in the present, let alone the future.

So what do we need to evaluate when interviewing someone for sixty minutes? And what can we say to the person who is interviewing us?

Well, if the interviewer understands our modern world and how technology has shaped it, then they would ask questions involving critical thinking. More than that, they would ask about problem-solving experience.

I think the most important thing is to know what the code is doing and understand how to troubleshoot and improve it. So scientific knowledge is a must and with that comes deep critical thinking. Philosophy and problem solving in all their modalities will be in massive need in the future.

This view is in the near future and "expecting horizon" but possibly in the far future we will not be in need to even this. So we need to keep up with the times and think about what skills are needed.

Bottom line, technology has created a job market and the kind of skills technical and non-technical people should have will depend on that. We are now living in a world where technology precedes the skills we need to work with it. It is paradoxical and circular, but in the same way as ethical frameworks (see chapter 8, New Technologies And Privacy (Or The Lack Of It)) we need to change the Cartesian maximum to "technologia ergo cogito ergo sum".

Skills like mathematics, logic and problem solving, which include critical thinking, are the most important when facing new technologies. How to test them in an interview is more of an art than a set of rules, but we need to change with the times and modify the way we approach our hunting for the skills we really need, not only from mere technology users but also from new generations of specialised technical people.

CHAPTER 20.
THIRTY Theory And Technical Designs

A civilization has the
ethics it can afford.

Larry Niven

Responsible AI: A philosophical approach is a must

There is much said about AI transparency and how automated algorithms took decisions based on "black boxes" and those instances when the AI's decisions had a significant impact in people's lives, there wasn't any real accountability.

But who is responsible here? The architect who designed the programme and chose the data? The data scientist who developed the algorithms? The managers who implemented the project? Well, maybe all of them are responsible for the consequences of AI implementations.

But in reality this is very difficult to assess and the problem of bias and ethical AI is a difficult one to solve.

Using the THIRTY theory as proposed in conjunction with Alec Boere, see [Plata, 2023], we can have a clearer outlook of the iterations AI can have in the near future. The theory states that we need to observe at least three iterations of a process to establish its long-term effects.

However, to foresee these iterations, we need to get involved in the design, development and execution of AI programmes and projects, which are complex and need to be thought of from many angles and perspectives.

From the ethical side, we normally see the first and most immediate consequences of AI initiatives, for example, making a supply chain system more efficient; that is obvious for everybody.

What is not normally seen are the consequences: optimising a process can bring psychological impacts to staff and workers, and social and economic ramifications might also be significant. But these effects are normally not immediate and so not considered when implementing AI programs. This is where the THIRTY theory is useful and should be considered in the technical design of any technical project or development.

Being responsible means that we need to think ethically about our work and proposals. But for that we need a logical or philosophical ground. Hence, we need to analyse the problem from a technical perspective and question even the scientific foundations as Henri Bergson [Bergson,1944] did with the theory of relativity.

In this sense, I see the problem like this:

Traditionally, AI is focused on the actual meaning of AI and its applications (see chapter 1 "Artificial Intelligence, What Do We Mean By That?"). Responsible AI is then condensed into the technical dimension, i.e. the man-machine relationship as stated by Norbert Wiener, one of the founders of Quantum Mechanics and pioneer of Cybernetics see [Wiener, 1965], in which the machine's processes are external to the human, the machine is in general outside the human reach even though its effects are inside people's lives (see the chapter 5, The Way We Relate With Machines).

Having a tick-box list which comes with a certification will put us in the traditional 18th century way of seeing ethical perspectives.

The THIRTY theory can shed light on the asymptotic effects of technology and its use. The analogy is computers-as-nice-type-writers versus computers-change-how-we-think-about-writing". This can only be seen after some iterations of the process.

If you accept that technologically driven domains dictate our ethical bearings by creating a structure or an architecture that define and delineate our actions as rule-bound, then technological developments are in themselves ecological, as we can see from many examples greatly developed in the work of Gregory Bateson [Bateson, 1972], where he suggests that ecology evolves according to the technical domain. In other words, the technical domain defines the ecological frame and not the other way around.

Now the question is "How can we comply with ecological norms if the compliance in itself is the norm?" Moreover, how can we build an ecological AI if AI is an ecology in and of itself?

Can you see that the problem of ethical AI gets very difficult very quickly? That is why if we really want to be ahead in responsible AI we need to evaluate our proposals and work as the critical conscience of our society.

The last thing we do is follow the ideas of cybernetics of the 1920s and the standards of traditional processes, or use an ethical programme based on administrative tasks, because then we would become judge, jury and executioner.

The future Chief Ethics Officer should be someone versed in philosophy, sociology, psychology and cultural studies primarily, plus they must be technically savvy and finally it would be useful if they were commercially driven. In that order of importance and not the other way around. In addition they need to understand science and technology thoroughly including the new scientific method (see chapter 7 "The Way We See Science").

Responsible AI requires a well thought strategy, an independent line of thought and thorough understanding of technical designs so we can see the ulterior consequences of technological developments. A theory that might work is the THIRTY, exposed in [Plata, 2023] that sustains that technology and their users work as a dynamical system that iterates over itself. And to see the effects of the system we need to observe at least three iterations. Finally, technological workers and developers will perform the role that universities used to have: be the social conscience of society.

CHAPTER 21.
The Way We See Marketing

I don't know half of you
half as well as I should like;
and I like less than half of you
half as well as you deserve.

J.R.R. Tolkien

Social media has become a major part of people's lives to connect with friends, family and colleagues or even help people find jobs, products and services.

I see people on public transport reading their social media feeds avidly. Even on long journeys they don't take their eyes off their cell phone screens. But why do we get so addicted to this?

Well, I am going with the Cyrenaic view and say that it is because it is pleasurable. We need to be aware that these platforms collect and store personal data and their algorithms uncover our preferences, which they record, monitor and measure in order to capture as much of our attention as they can.

And this is one of the things that technology changed about marketing: Modern marketing is about attention.[18] To get more of our attention, marketers and technologists used a so-called intermittent reinforcement.

There is a vast amount of research done on this topic, and how it is related to manipulation, and abusive relationships but at its core it is about delivering rewards or penalties at irregular or random intervals. In the marketing case we label it as a positive, so it is a "positive intermittent reinforcement" see [Hogarth 2010].

_____

18 For more see article in Marketing Week by Mark Ritson [Ritson, 2022]

There is a bio-chemical component to this reinforcement, the so-called instant gratification. When one has gratification, one secretes dopamine in the brain, giving us a pleasurable sensation, which can be very addictive, see [Kancel, 2016].

This is also applied to video games. The gaming industry knows this really well. The player receives just enough rewards at the appropriate points to encourage them to continue playing (see the chapter 11 "The Way We Work").

As with any addiction, rewards must get faster and faster. If one has longer intermittent stimuli in the brain the addiction can be more controllable, but not at the pace at which technology forces us to respond.

At a personal level, scrolling on TikTok is so addictive! People cannot wait to scroll to have the next dopamine shot, attributing to this, the short attention span of the younger generations. But I think it is not only newer generations but everybody, as it is a chemical reaction in the brain. If the older generation is not affected by it, then likely it is because they are not social media.

Creating these reactions in the brain are not preceded by the creation of a new or better thing that piques or impresses the viewer – but by a different thing. I think we like the stimulus of something different and possibly technology will make new generations addicted to change. For example, the number of divorces and polyamour relationships are on the rise[19] and it is not that someone cheating on an intimate partner does it for someone richer or younger or more attractive, but just for someone different.

---

19 This is debatable based on how we see statistics, but for reference see [Wilkinson & Finkbeiner, 2024]

The same happens with technology. It is not necessarily the innovative but the difference in the short term, and following Nicholas of Cusa in his "coincidentia oppositorum", many little different things will become a big innovative one.

Technology drives dopamine and endorphin through rapid changes and different things that make us feel pleasure and get us addicted. Marketers are more interested in getting our attention than putting products or trends in our heads and use new technologies to procure that attention from us. We need to understand the role of these substances in the brain and be aware of how technology is used on us as consumers.

.

CHAPTER 22.
The Way We Write

A writer is someone who has
taught his mind to misbehave.

Oscar Wilde

One of the things I observe from popular tech platforms is the lack of argumentation. Modern technologies force us to express our ideas in a limited number of characters. For X (formerly Twitter) it used to be 140 characters (not words, characters) and it increased to 280 characters in 2017, I guess due to the need of elaboration.

When we elaborate ideas, for example, this one that I am writing here, I am surely exceeding 280 characters because I have to expand a logical argument, that is, I have to show research and facts, and then explain it in a comprehensive way and not only with a shallow comment like, "I don't like it" or "I think you are right". Other technologies allow short comments and blogs so posts are longer but dynamically they are similar: a soundbite versus a paragraph.

But elaborating ideas and laying out concepts requires a narrative, argumentation and solid rhetoric. Which is very difficult to achieve in short paragraphs or in sentences of 280 characters.

The way we write is now changing. Even this book is written in a way that I would have never imagined. My other books are written in a more traditional style, where I develop an argument and express ideas with a certain rhetoric and cadence, explaining thoroughly the thought process and conclusions. Not this one. Following my own ideas, I changed! I modified my way of writing with the modern times and technology.

And even when I am writing in a more succinct, concise and to-the-point manner it is imperative that I elaborate on concepts, show serious research and convey a clear message to the reader. The result should be same: these lines should trigger a meditation and reflection on the ideas.

Technology runs really fast and a post on a blog, a post on X (formerly a tweet) or a comment on any other platform must be quickly done. Relevance is a thing measured now by the speed of comments. And at some point even conversations or threads are closed after a certain period of time, so they have expiry dates, and after that, we cannot continue the discussion or follow up on ideas.

Obviously ideas cannot be too controversial otherwise they get censored and canceled, and it is not because they are controversial, but because there is a lack of elaboration which leads to a lack of context. If a comment is taken out of context, then there is a communication problem.

These platforms are leading us to, at best, building an argument through small collective paragraphs, a process that I do not agree with.

The way we write meaningful ideas should have other channels if we really want to maintain control over the narrative, both in broad strokes and also in the detail of its logic. Without this, we do not reach the depth of knowledge and level of discussion needed to develop further ideas but in a more constructive and concise way at the same time.

Not long ago I came across a very interesting book by a graphic designer, Jessica Wynee, who published an art book about the blackboards of mathematicians. Yes, blackboards like in the old days when we used to write with chalks. But the interesting proposal was that the act of writing with chalk forces the mind to slow down and thus to find new concepts at a pace conducive to understanding, see [Wynee, 2021].

Being in front of a blackboard makes collaboration easier than with a computer screen. There are no glitches or errors that can prevent the ideas flowing out. And it forces a cerebral discipline into the physical realm. This is very good from the epistemic point of view. So maybe writing in the old way, on a piece of paper, is a good thing for knowledge and thinking.

But now, with technologies that transcribe audio into text, we can actually dictate our thoughts. Not even do we not need to type our ideas on a keyboard but just talk, which goes hand in hand with lack of mental processes of slowing down to look for understanding, GenAI platforms can help us with rephrasing and being concise. Having these available all the time (in our phones) may lead to a real change in the way we write.

Technologies are forcing us to write fast, think fast, and sometimes not think well. Carl Sagan, the famous scientist known for his popularising book and TV series Cosmos, said that humans are not good at thinking fast, but certainly at thinking well. So maybe it would be good to slow down every now and then, grab a piece of paper and write our ideas with a pen

CHAPTER 23.
Chaos In The Modern World

Our real discoveries come from chaos,
from going to the place that
looks wrong and stupid and foolish.

Chuck Palahniuk

Chaos in physics is defined as the property of a complex system whose behavior is so unpredictable as to appear random. In mathematics, it is defined as a system that has great sensitivity to small changes in its initial conditions.

Given these definitions, we can say that we live in a chaotic world that we just cannot control. We think we have control over our world, but due to the huge number of variables needed to control reality, we just do not have any control over it. We react to chaotic stimuli from the world and deal with a series of actions. That is pretty much what we can do.

Chaos traditionally is contrary to order. And we used to say that a well ordered system or world is not chaotic, and rules, like cause-and-effect, are well known and established.

But chaos from an AI point of view is equivalent to probability. Many machine-learning algorithms are based on random probabilistic models and even GenAI has a strong probabilistic component.

So we can say that in our modern world, the contrary to chaos is "the necessary" and not the well-ordered, in the same way, the opposite of probable is not improbable but certain.

Fate is a given property of an ordered world and that is what philosophers call deterministic. In other words, fate is predetermined and is to happen for sure or with certainty. Usual examples are the inevitable death (sorry to be so grim), but also if you use your car you will eventually have to change tires; we cannot specify when but for sure you will have to change them as long as you use the car.

So why do we say that the world is in chaos if the opposite argument is equally true, that all is predetermined and meant to happen (like changing tires)?

Well, because we have both conditions at the same time. In the long term the probability of something happening is almost sure (like the example of the tires), but in the short term, the probabilities are absolutely impossible to determine. In the short term, our actions also affect the short term outcomes, but in the long run, probabilities are so high that the outcome seems almost sure.

So, in our postmodern technological world there is a short term and a long term view of the world and both are equally valid. The long term is deterministic: we approach the inevitable outcome, like death. But this is always in the long term. The short term on the other hand is probabilistic and random (chaotic).

An example in physics is the alpha decay of radioactive particles, which follow a well known differential equation (differential equations are deterministic), but in the short term they also follow a probability distribution (the Poisson distribution, which is chaotic) and both are correct!

There is an important exception. If you do sufficient actions in one direction, then the probabilities of something happening in that direction are higher. This is possible only with the fast implementation of actions and automations with technology.

There are two views of the world, one probabilistic or chaotic in the short term and the other certain or deterministic in the long term. Technology like GenAI shows us that random variations in the micro world (or quantum if you will) are more visible than expected variations at the macro level.

CHAPTER 24.
Do People Change Or Is It Just Technology?

Everyone thinks of changing the world,
but no one thinks of changing himself.

Leo Tolstoy

I will try to reflect now on an old question "do people change?" from a modern technological point of view.

One answer I would like to go with is that people don't change, people adapt to circumstances. We think they change but the thing that changes is the context and people only adjust to it.

My brother always told me, "In case of doubt read the classics". So I will follow Aristippus of Cyrene and Epicurus on hedonistic philosophy. Hedonism insists that the ultimate goal of humans is pleasure. Moreover, Cyrenaics, like Atristippus, adds that pleasure is immediate and local (see the chapter 21 "The Way We See Marketing").

In summary, hedonism explain human actions by looking for pleasure and avoiding pain. My argument follows this premise and I say that humans reshape to circumstances that will lead them to avoid pain or seek for pleasure.

Some can argue that there is an exception here: what about the masochists. I would reply that masochists are contradictory as they find pleasure in pain, so in the end they also fall into the pleasure-seeking theory.

There is however a possible exception: athletes. They do not avoid pain but manage it; that is why they often injure themselves. Our bodies naturally tell us when to stop, and how do they do that? Through pain; when we feel physical pain, our bodies are telling us to "stop". But athletes, even when they feel pain, keep going regardless.

Now remember that pleasure is comfort and, due to technology, we live in a society of comfort. The philological[20] principle of least effort applies also to normal life and all aspects of it, mainly through providing comfort, and technology drives us to the least expensiture of effort (which is pain avoidance, although the pain is more of nuisance) and that is pleasurable in and of itself, but also because we have more time to ourselves and for our desire for pleasure.

In this sense, being idle comes first and getting busy is a necessity to survive. But when we finish our main needs to survive, being idle and enjoying ourselves is immediately next. People look for this inevitably as it is in human's nature to do it. Technology helps humans to have more time to be idle. The negation of idleness is business. This is clear in other languages like Spanish, where "ocio" means idle and "negocio" means business is the negation of it: "negocio" is "nec-ocio" or the negation of idleness.[21]

Business and technology are closely related. Humans are also technical by nature and they change their environment as soon as they can to have pleasure. The adjustment to different circumstances is just a temporary transition state towards technology. And the use of technology assists with the transition to a more pleasurable environment.

---

20 Philology is the field that studies the structure, history and evolution of language.
21 For more on this argument and technique and its philosophical consequences, see the work of Ortega y Gasset.

Here's a lovely example: The ancient civilisation of Sumer had a surplus of food and needed to track inventory and trade, So it invented our first texts as a tool to assist with accounting. Sumerians took that tool and immediately wrote something to give themselves pleasure: an epic story of love and battle called Gilgamesh. They could have written texts about how to build a palace or dig a ditch or of philosophy or religion. But no, they preferred the pleasure of a page turner.

In conclusion people don't change, they are the same and they look for the same: comfort and pleasure; and this is more obvious with technological advancements as it is the technology around them that changes the circumstance and they only adjust to it temporarily.

In general people look for comfort and idleness because it is pleasurable (this is the hedonistic philosophical principle), and technology is the vehicle to have more time to be idle. When we say that people change, in reality they don't; it is more the circumstance around them that changes, and what we observe is merely a temporary adaptation to this change. Technology emphasises this and in the end, humans being technical, they will change their circumstance.

CHAPTER 25.
Human Beings Are Historical Beings

We are not makers of history.
We are made by history.

Martin Luther King, Jr.

Why do I say that humans are historical in essence? The present is so ephemeral that it ceases to exist in an instant. In fact, what you are reading now is already in the past. While you read, the light is reflected on these lines, which go into your eyes. This takes time (even fractions of a second, but remember that a fraction of a second is already in the past), and this is not taking into account the fact that there is a further process for you to realise that you read these lines: from the perception of light in your eyes, there is a neural impulse that goes to your brain to decode those symbols, your brain in turn interprets (based on your cultural background and previous experience) what those symbols mean, followed by a further impulse which indicates the realisation of reading and finally verbalising the written words, "I am reading right now".

All these steps take time, so what you were actually reading is already in the past even as you say, "I am doing it right now".

The conversation that we have with others does not have its value in what it was but what it represented to us in our memories (see chapter 14 "Technology And Memory"). In that sense we always talk about the past. The way to make sense of it is through history.

I am not going to explain historiographical theories, but one of the main factors that differentiate history from "the past" is that history has a context and an angle (the historian's angle). For a good introduction to historiography see [Gilderhus, 2002].

In this sense, We are historians of our own life.

And I would like to stress the word historical and not "of the past". History requires an interpretation and it is used to explain our current responses. Living in the past would not allow us to respond to new stimuli from the world, but being historical forms our conscience.

History is personal and – I would say – inherently biased. Try to remember what your aunt or sister or someone close to you said in a family reunion 10 years ago. It is impossible to quote word by word (unless you have eidetic memory), but what we do remember is tones, gestures, some words and the general atmosphere of those words, for example, she was angry or happy and she said something like "I don't like the coffee". Which is a very vague account of the real events, which are full of details like colors and precise words.

Even when we talk to friends we talk about the past: the book you read, the movie you saw, what happened at work or your views on something (which is already in the past). We get that our selective memory and the way we articulate it is precisely the historical part.

But technology has changed all that. Humans tend to be "past beings" now and not "historical" ones. Thanks to huge databases, having extensive memory of video and audio of ourselves is extremely easy and even cheap. Surveillance systems and mobile technologies of all sorts catch images and actions of employees, public figures and normal citizens from all angles and from all devices.

With our phones we can recall immediately the exact words and gestures of past events. The problem I see with this is that we lose the context, we lose who we are because we are our own historical recount.

We are historical beings because we have a personal angle and view of events, which might be lost due to the constant data memory that technology keeps. Video will not capture our emotions or state of mind at the time as we say something. This is why our own history gives us our personal context that only people close to us would understand (see chapter 8 "New Technologies And Privacy (Or The Lack Of It)").

And how about the future? Now the future has not happened. The future is pure speculation and the farther you go into the future, the more imprecise the speculation is.

There is an obsession with knowing the future, but this is only to control the chaos and the probabilistic world in which we live (see chapter 23 "Chaos In The Modern World"). Due to the amount of information we receive every day from our technological devices like cell phones, our feeds from social media platforms and electronic communications, we only allow ourselves to speculate in the near future or what the philosopher Paul Ricoeur calls the "expecting horizon".

The far future is so uncertain due to constant changes of information in the ephemeral present that new generations think in the short term. I see that the "expecting horizon" or near future is the actual future in our modern world. The future as such is hollowed out and the past, which should be full of emotions and thoughts, is reduced to data memory. As a result, the possibilities to reshape ourselves by analysing it are narrowed.

One human feature is to be historical. Yet technology is turning humans into past beings more than historical beings. Context is lost if we have a constant memory of events stored as data available for recall at any time. But this is only dehumanising us. Future is only the expecting horizon, and the far future is so uncertain that it is hollow as a concept.

CHAPTER 26.
The Only Way To Stay In The Present Is Art

Forever is composed of nows.

Emily Dickinson

As said in chapter 25 "Human Beings Are Historical Beings", our natural place is always in the past, the future is constant speculation and the present is so ephemeral that it is already gone. Being in the present or future is equivalent to being out of our natural place. So how can we experience the present if our place is in the past?

Following the theologian Gilbert Meilaender in his book, *The Limits of Love*, sexual intercourse is "the act in which human beings are present most fully". This idea was already proposed by Augustine in his *Confessions* in the 3rd century, but I decided to use the revisited idea in a more modern language.

Following this idea, the only way of not thinking about the future or any consequences that our actions will have, and at the same time also not caring about any memories is when we are in ecstasy. In fact the word "ecstasy" can be separated in two parts: ex meaning out and stasis meaning place which leads to the meaning "out of place".

If our natural place is history (as humans are historical beings) and the past and our thoughts toward the chaos of the world are in the future, then the only place we are not at in any moment of time is in the present.

Now, the epitome of ecstasy is the sexual one, and following Meilaender's idea, when humans are in sexual ecstasy, they do not think about the past, and they do not speculate on what will happen in the future. At that moment they are in the pure present: there are no thoughts, no ideas or events to process, no speculation of thoughts about consequences or ripple effects. The only thing at the moment of ecstasy is the moment itself and the person in it. That is what I would call "being in the pure present".

But let's extrapolate this idea to other types of ecstasy: when we read a poem, see a painting or listen to music there might be a moment of ecstasy. A circumstance that extracts us from any thoughts and deems us oblivious of any consequence, speculation or remembrance. That is a pure present experience or what Aristotle calls transcendence.

All these examples of pure present are related to art and that is why it is so important to keep our artistic endeavors alive. It is a vehicle to experience pure present.

Art is about beauty, and beauty is related to the philosophical term "aesthetics" and after exploring some of different definitions of beauty, I agree with Arthur Schopenhauer who argues that beauty is "something that seizes our will". If our will is no more, then the only thing left is our pure emotion. Our will is our capacity of rationalising but in the presence of beauty, for example a painting, a ballet, a music concert or another human being we might consider beautiful, then our logic is gone, and we might do the most irrational things that in hindsight might look crazy.

Art is related to this, and triggers emotions in us, moreover, by enhancing our emotions until we reach states of ecstasy. And this is precisely the connection.

Art is created by humans. But with technology, this is changing. In fact, the artwork of this same book was developed by a human using AI tools. The reader will decide if this appeals to them or not, but in the randomness of AI combined with the views of an artist there might be an image or a sound that really lifts us mentally and emotionally from our natural place and takes us to the pure present.

Now, being in the pure present might be even easier and more powerful due to technology and the availability to create art in the sense of aesthetics.

One thing is certain: technology is triggering emotions in humans, be it through the generation of images or by creating sounds or poems.

Being in the pure present will be a more common thing in the future. Will this be good or bad? No way to tell now. The trend seems to be for creatives to use technology instead of brushes or pencils (even electronic pencils). Machines can help create ideas for artists looking for new ways of taking people out of their natural places.

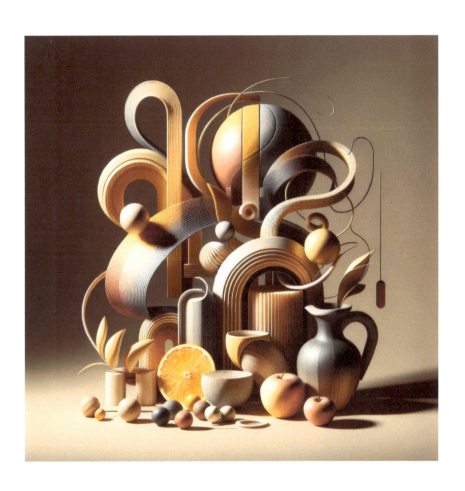

CHAPTER 27.
The Real Present With Modern Technology?

You got a lifetime. No more. No less.

Neil Gaiman

This is an epilogue from the previous two chapters.

There is a concept in physics called the light cone. This is a cone expanding at the speed of light and, as nothing can go faster than the speed of light, every possible event in the universe is inside the cone. Outside the cone are all those impossible events as nothing can exceed the speed of light.

One immediate connection to this is that sometimes we worry about things that are outside the light cone. Well, not exactly … but we worry about things that are at the edge of the cone and have a very low probability of happening. This is natural and many self-help books dwell on the idea of not thinking about those events and concentrating on what is important and have more probability of happening. Even Stephen Covey in his famous book *7 habits of highly effective people* mentions a technique to focus on our circle of influence, which is our immediate and personal light cone.

The light cone is connected to being historical. The philosopher Gilles Deleuze shows us that not only does the cone expand to the future but also to the past. As human beings, it is impossible to contemplate all the possible events that can be or could have been. Instead we have selective memory and – what I call – historical accounts of the past events.

Present in this diagram of the cone is the exact vertex. The singular point where the lines of the cone intersect. This point is constantly moving and it is precisely that: a point, hence the ephemeral property of it.

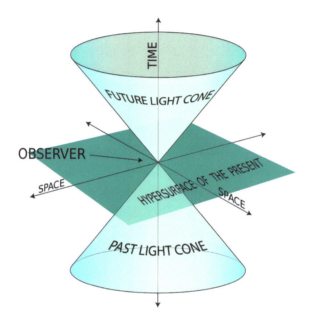

Image taken from: [World line.svg]

In practical terms, as explained in the previous chapters, the future is only speculation and our vision of the future is immediate. The only thing we can see in the future is what the philosopher Paul Ricoeur calls the "expecting horizon". This is the immediate future and where I think reality is.

The real world is not what it is because – as said before – it is so ephemeral that is already in the past; the pure present can only be achieved by disconnecting from past and future.

So what we really are is what we are in the process of being, in other words our becoming in the expecting horizon.

The future is so full of possibilities that the only ones with high probability of happening are those in this short-term future inside the cone. And this is what chaotic systems are in practical human terms (see chapter 23 "Chaos In The Modern World").

As we live in the expecting horizon, we can change direction at any time so we change our future perspective according to our actions in "the becoming".

What we call the present is nothing else but the vertex of the light cone that constantly moves in time. What we really are is what we are becoming as we live in the expecting horizon. People are not what they did or used to be, neither are they what they plan to be in the future, but what they are in the process of being; the phrase "i am what i am becoming" should make sense out of this discussion and as an epilogue of the previous chapters.

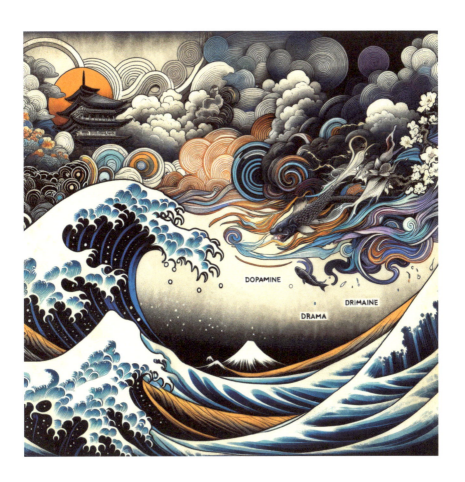

CHAPTER 28.
Humans Being Are Dramatic Beings

I never travel without my diary.
One should always have something
sensational to read in the train.

Oscar Wilde

Since the dawn of time there has been some sort of oral tradition which safeguarded communal stories. The first written "history" seems to be that of Herodotus who is considered the father of history. While all his "historical" stories are engaging and explain how the world was created along with other stories of heroes and gods, some of his stories have considerable accuracy.

Many years ago, storytellers in tribes were of the utmost importance, not only to maintain traditions, but also to bring something that humans needed: drama.

But what is drama? Drama is the literary genre that enhances emotions, be it sadness, happiness or any other. The point of drama is to hype emotions and feelings.

Storytellers are experts in bringing drama to our imagination. It is not the same to say, They went to the mountains, killed a beast and returned." As it is to say, "They went to the mountains and at night they heard a growl that scared them like never before and they saw those red eyes looking at them with fiercely hatred… etc". Drama is about storytelling.

Our modern life is full of routines, and that makes them dull and boring: we get up, go to work which is frequently routine and then go back home. Rinse and repeat. When something out of the ordinary happens on the way to work like a demonstration or a burst water main or sadly an accident, people want to stay and look on. When they go home they say, "Guess what happened today?"

That is adding drama to their already tedious lives.

And then there's the weekend. We dress up and go out. But why? To meet people? Dance, drink? Deep down, what we are looking for is drama. Meeting a boy or a girl in a nightclub is drama! Being dumped by someone is drama! Having an affair is drama! Being in love is drama, even being in danger is drama! We like drama! It is the salt of life! With no drama there is no life and nothing worthy of telling.

Hormones like dopamine and endorphins are dramatic. When we secrete those hormones, we are full of emotions, in other words, we feel drama.

But where does technology fit in? A friend of mine told me she was on Instagram only to see but not to be seen; she did not post anything but she liked to see other's posts. But why? Let's keep applying our drama theory.

If we classify the types of social media users with respect to the drama they like, I would find three different categories: anonymously seeing, anonymously being seen, and being seen by known people.

The first likes to hear stories and is considered to be the audience of the storyteller. The second is those who participate in comments based on others' posts. This attitude brings them closer to the drama, but not as close as being at the center of it. I understand why teenage novels adapted to films are so popular. They bring drama, but not too much to feel horrified, threatened or in danger.

Each human being needs a specific amount of drama and that is why in technology platforms we have a number of people commenting on posts: trolling, agreeing or simply putting neutral comments, all sorts of levels. Allowing comments is the best way to achieve personalised amounts of drama.

And finally the third group, which are those who post. These are the most dramatic of all and are equivalent to the storytellers.

The problem is that, in the iterations of more and more dramatic content, we are exposing more and more intimate details (see chapter 20 "THIRTY Theory And Technical Designs"). It seems that people are sharing more and more intimate moments and experiences. Just the other day I was watching on TikTok someone crying bitterly about something that happened to her and another who was dumped by the girlfriend telling the story in a rather humiliating way, etc.

Drama needs to grow in intensity and has to be believable. Perhaps that is why people show their intimate side so we think "it must be true". Some politicians getting emotional in front of the cameras when attacked is one of the trends of "look at my drama, I also suffer like you", which might not be true at all but works like a shot on dopamine drama. In a way, they are playing the part of the storyteller by putting some drama in the story.

Technology allows us to access drama and more people are posting their lives and even their more intimate moments. Influencers and active users of social platforms are leveling up their game by posting more dramatic stories and ever more intimate things. Where will this go? What do you think, dear reader?

CHAPTER 29.
The Chip They Inserted In Our Brain: Personal Inertia

Belief gets in the way of learning.

Robert A. Heinlein

They (and by they I mean society, friends, parents) put so much stuff in our heads. Most of it is for a good reason, like looking both ways before crossing the street, achieving your goals and avoiding things that might be detrimental for individuals and society.

But there are rules that just make no sense or are simply outdated for the purpose they were created. This is what I call a "chip in our brain", like a computer chip that controls the actions of the computer.

Have you thought why is it that normal working hours are from nine to five? Why don't we start our workday at six in the morning? The question is, Why do we still have a work week that is Monday to Friday, midmorning to late afternoon? Is it practical? Given technological advancements, I work different schedules[22] and I have learnt that very capable people work odd hours. Why should we try to control this?

There are still companies and managers who think traditionally and force people to be in the office at certain hours like in the 19th

---

22 In fact, in technology and data teams it has been a common practice for many years to work remotely; I remember doing this 15 years ago. Now, thanks to technological tools, it is more common to have remote teams of all sorts across many time zones. And modern managers have adjusted their working styles to this.

century. I think it's to control their staff more than controlling the output they generate. These old-school managers and companies are the last ones to adopt technology and consequently change.

Foucault in his book on panopticism tells us about control over people and tells us cases about car factories and how his theory applies; and yes, many rules were aimed for controlling women in the past. Remaining a virgin until matrimony was a blatant sexual control that add nothing to the person, relationships or broader society. This rule applied widely to women but not to men, which enhances not only the hypocrisy but the fact that it was about controlling.

If we control others' endorphins and others' drama, then we control them (see chapter 28 "Humans Beings Are Dramatic Beings"). If we tell them how they can have their drama and how they cannot, we have complete our power over them.

Work and our output should be enjoyable and our output even at work should have a pleasurable component that can push people to be creative and do their best in what they do. But tradition is powerful. Maybe ideas from older generations coming from ascetic societies in Europe are telling us back in our heads that work should not be pleasurable.

Hedonism should be free and not controlled. But that chip is very powerful! When we "misbehaved" we have an immediate response from the chip in our brains saying, "That is wrong". Even when some things do not make sense for us, the chip indicates the opposite.

People who do not want to get married end up in horrible situations. Why? Because getting married was the "correct" thing to do. It was the next step in life. Study in university, get a job, get married, have children … all milestones for the chip that forces us to complete them.

And all those milestones are so ephemeral! Once you have your university degree, that emotion lasts a day. The day you get married is a day, and the rest of life is the consequence of that and that is not the milestone but sometimes a cross to bear.

In the past a spinster was stigmatised, women without children were looked down upon or pitied. But once we liberate ourselves from the yoke of the chip, we can live our lives happily and more consciously, really acting on what we really want or need, and not something that was imposed subconsciously to us.

Technology is helping us to liberate ourselves from traditions due to the amount of information available. However change is not always easy and immediate. We need to process change, and that is why this book can help us realise how the speed of the modern world and technology is affecting us as human beings in our most usual activities like business, love and outlook on the world. Most important is to identify old inertia and "the chip in the brain" and change it if we want to.

CHAPTER 30.
Poetry And Love And Technology

If everyone is thinking alike,
then no one is thinking.

Benjamin Franklin

This is a summary that will serve as a wrap up of all chapters.

One of the points covered in the previous chapters was the impact of technology on our relationships with others, and specially the marital ones. Perhaps because we can see that a lot of other people are getting divorced, it is not a stigma anymore, and also because we want more drama (see chapter 28 "Humans Beings Are Dramatic Beings"), technology is re-shaping our intimate life. Is it that dating apps give us the dopamine hit that comes with different things (in this case, people), like video games and marketing?

Does this mean that the future is polyamoruros relationships or an endless churn of new partners? Let's make a quick reflection on why this might be and what is provoking this modern and more technological love in the era of information.

There are two poems that tell us about life and relationships. The first one is Elizabeth Barrett Browning 'If Thou Must Love Me, Let It Be for Naught'

If thou must love me, let it be for nought
Except for love's sake only. Do not say
I love her for her smile … her look … her way
Of speaking gently,

Beautiful way to put it. Love should not have a reason, but should happen for compulsion. Why do we fall in love, not for a reason at all, but because we are compelled. Or Barrett Browning put it, "Love for love's sake." But compulsion comes with endorphins or dopamine (see chapter 24 "Do People Change Or Is It Just Technology?"); it is irrational and leads to drama for the sake of it! That is love!

But in the same way that love is compelled, it fades away. This poem is precisely about killing the chip! (see chapter 29 "The Chip They Inserted In Our Brain: Personal Inertia") It is not about any reason, for being handsome or having a good social position, etc. no, it is the most irrational impulse. And that has to do with all what I said in previous chapters, about beauty and volition, drama and hormones in the brain, and also about the way we see the world through the lens of technology, e.g. pure past and living in the expecting horizon (see chapter 27 "The Real Present With Modern Technology?" and chapter 25 "Human Beings Are Historical Beings").

In this sense, lovemaking without love is just making … Well, the argument is that lovemaking without love leads to pure pleasure. It is ecstasy in its purest form (see chapter 25 "Human Beings Are Historical Beings"). There is nothing apart from the actual act, hence the possibility of experiencing pure present though it (see chapter 26 The Only Way To Stay In The Present Is Art"). And perhaps technological tools and apps can facilitate this lovemaking without love, especially in the younger generations.

The other poem is William Blake's 'The sick rose'

O Rose thou art sick.
The invisible worm,
That flies in the night
In the howling storm:

Has found out thy bed
Of crimson joy:
And his dark secret love
Does thy life destroy.

Many scholars have discussed the meaning and significance of the "worm", that worm that flies in the night in the howling storm and destroys life or love. Some say it is jealousy, others envy or another lover, and others think that it is love that destroys itself.

I think the worm is tedium. Tedium is invisible but we all know it well. You don't know when or why but suddenly everything in a human social environment becomes stale, be it a personal relationship or work or our technological gadgets. Tedium finds the bed of crimson joy (passion) and destroys it! (see chapter 28, Humans Being Are Dramatic Beings)

Tedium kills drama, the day-to-day routine is the one that kills love and because of love happening by compulsion, "rationale" does not come into play. Avoiding tedium and looking for drama in life is a choice of hedonists. And in a modern society with its constant information feeds, change is encouraged at an accelerated pace and technological market cycles force us into a rather aggressive way to have new or "different" products.

There is a song by the band "No Doubt" where famous singer Gwen Stefani used to sing; the name of the song is "New" and the song starts with:

Don't let it go away
This feeling has got to stay
Don't let it go away
This feeling has got to stay
And I can't believe I've had this chance now
Don't let it go away, yeah

New, you're so new
You, you're new
And I never had this taste in the past
New, you're so new

Think for a moment why is it that we always look for new experiences, such as new places that we have not yet visited. Even children on Christmas like to have a "new something".

Now there is a reflection on this: We like new things. But why? Because we like drama. In fact following from an idea by Ann-Christine Duhaime in her piece at the Harvard Business Review,[23] humans are hard wired to like or even to need novelty.

With respect to technology we like new gadgets and want to try all of them and that is why fast innovation is of the utmost importance in our modern world. And as said by Michael Crichton in one of his amazing novels, quoting the Red Queen in Alice in Wonderland, we need to run as fast as we can so we stay in the same place that we are.

If we are in the cutting edge of innovation and technology and we want to keep that edge (being in the same position), then we need to run as fast as we can just to keep up with the speed of technology. Love is not an exception and I can see that even love is affected by technology in a meaningful way.

---

23 Duhaime Ann-Christine, Our Brains Love New Stuff, and It's Killing the Planet, Harvard Business Review, March 2017

With respect to technological advancements and their usage, we do not like something new or something better. On many occasions we want something different. Dopamines in the modern world do not consider something new or an improvement, which at the speed that people need stimuli would be unsustainable. However, something different would suffice. Possibly this explains the explosion of dating apps and the new view of love. This is clearly reflected in the uncomfortable reality that post-industrial capitalism, which is heavily influenced by the success of appealing to that dopamine hit. So there's fast fashion. There's TikTok and social media. Marketing is based around that dopamine hit. It's not just that we are naturally inclined towards novelty, it's that the brain's hard wiring for novelty is being enhanced by social media to need more novelty than before. And like all drugs, the hit is less of a hit and so the need is greater than before. This is our economic system, of which technology gadgets play no small part.

So the Red Queen's statement in the view of new technologies, should change to, "We don't need to run to stay in the same place, but we just need to run faster".

EPILOGUE.
Art With AI

Even a couple of years ago, it was said that all creative work, especially art, could not be replaced by machines. And of course there is a strong component of human interaction in creating art, but the fact that this book has all its artwork done by an artist working with the assistance of AI tools is proof that we have reached a milestone in technology and art.

My dear editor, Dr. Katie Isbester, told me that she remembered once reading a book on the history of language and its connection to the industrial revolution. The argument was that mechanisation required homogenisation of time, spelling, language usage and so on which relates to Max Weber's bureaucratisation of the state and society.

Before then, no one was overly fussed if you spelled your name however you felt, invented words willy-nilly, and changed existing spellings. The printing press imposed standardisation on publishing. This includes things like the placement of pictures.

This technology has changed again and we are no longer bound by standardization. Hence the use of images in this book in new and unusual ways. So the design of the book reflects my argument that the tool makes the difference.

What we (Nelly, the illustrator, and I) would like to write in this section is our experience using technology to create this book.

I have not used any AI tool to write any part of this book and all the ideas and concepts in here are based on my experience and research. By which I mean is that I did not use ChatGPT or other GenAI tools to write any part of the book. However, as this was a book about seeing the world in a different way due to technology and AI, I decided to participate with an artist who is creating art with AI and include her work in this book.

And what a great way to do it but with artwork for each chapter. Nelly has been working on plastic art and photography for years now, always thriving for avant-garde topics, testing materials, textures and techniques mainly in the abstract style. So she showed us that different styles in this book and other subsequent books will be a good space for creatives to express ideas alongside other disciplines.

Nelly wanted to try new techniques as she has been exploring the capabilities of AI in art, and proposed her own designs for this book but with the assistance of AI, specifically Dall-E.

Her experience was gratifying with the results, but in her own words, "we need to work more on this and keep iterating with technology to get better results." She continued, "I think we are in a breakthrough in exploring a brand-new technique and very useful tools, which will lead to a plethora of new designs, styles and concepts".

All the art in this book is subject to the Content Policy and OpenAI Terms, so Nelly owns the images that she create with DALL·E, including the right to reprint, sell, and merchandise. For more guidelines on how to refer to art with technology see

https://help.openai.com/en/articles/6425277-can-i-sell-images-i-create-with-dall-e

My wish is that this book stirs some thoughts, provokes reflections on many concepts, triggers some curiosity and gets people to be closer to technology. But mainly I wish the reader to enjoy the book, its art and ideas. Just be hedonist about it and connect emotionally and intellectually. And paraphrasing the Red Queen, I hope this book will help us running as fast as we can to end up in a different place through new ways of thinking and seeing ourselves.

REFERENCES

Alvesson M., Spicer A., *A stupidity-based theory of organizations*, Journal of management studies, j.1567-6486.2012.01072.x, 2012

Altoe F., Joyner D., *Annotation-free Automatic Examination Essay Feedback Generation*, IEEE Learning With MOOCS (LWMOOCS) pp 110-115, Georgia Institute of Technology, 2019

Aristotle, *The complete works of Aristotle*, Bollingen; 71:2, Barnes Jonathan, Princeton university Press, Princeton New Jersey, 1984

Barthes R., *Elements of Semiology*, Hill and Wang, New York, 1986

Bateman A., Bonanni L., *What Supply Chain Transparency Really Means* Harvard Business Review, Cambridge Massachusetts, August 2019

Bateson G., *Steps to an ecology of the mind*, Chandler Publishing Company, Toronto, 1972

Bergson H., *Creative Evolution*, Translated by Arthur Miychell, Random House, New York, 1944

Blackman R., *A Practical Guide to Building Ethical AI*, Harvard Business Review, Cambridge Massachusetts, October 2020

Canaparo Caludoi, *The manufacture of an author : Reinaldo Arenas's literary world, his readers and other contemporaries*, King's College London, 2000

Canaparo Claudio, *Geo-Epistemology*, Peter Lang, Bern, 2009

Clark Kim B., Wheelwright Steven C., *Organizing and Leading "Heavyweight" Development Teams*, California Management Review, Volume 34, Issue 3, 1992

Crichton M., *Jurassic Park*, Alfred A. Knopf, New York, 1990

Christensen C. R. , Andrews K.R..Bower J. L., Hammermesh G. and Porter M.E. *Business Policy, Text and Cases*, 5th Edition, Homewood, IL, Irwin, 1982

Christensen C. M., Overdorf M., *Meeting the Challenge of Disruptive Change*, Harvard Business Review, March 2000

Data Science Central 2019, *The Typical Data Scientist Profile*, available at https://www.datasciencecentral.com/profiles/blogs/the-typical-data-scientist-profile-in-2019 accessed 29/02/2024

Descartes R., *Discourse on Method and Meditations on First Philosophy*, translated by Donald A Cress, Hackett Publishing Company, Indianapolis, Cambridge, 1998

Deleuze G., Guattari F., *What is Philosophy?*, translated by Hugh Tomlinson, Columbia University Press, 1994

De Saussure F., *Course of General Linguistics*, translated by Wade Baskin, Columbia University Press, New York, 1959

Duhaime Ann-Christine, *Our Brains Love New Stuff, and It's Killing the Planet*, Harvard Business Review, March 2017

Feyerabend Paul, *Against Method*, New Left Books, London, 1975

G20 Digital Economy Task Force, 2021, *Measuring Artificial Intelligence in Official Statistics*

DETF workshop, *Session 2* available at https://unstats.un.org/ unsd/nationalaccount/aeg/2021/M15_7_3_AI_Issue_Note.pdf accessed on 26/02/2024

George M.L, *The Lean Six Sigma Pocket Toolbook: A Quick Reference Guide to 100 Tools for Improving Quality and Speed*, McGraw-Hill; 1st Edition, London, 2005
Guardian, 2018, https://www.theguardian.com/ technology/2018/aug/21/the-undertakers-of-silicon-valley-how-failure-became-big-business accessed on 19/02/2024

Hogarth Robin, Villeval Marie-Claire, *Intermittent Reinforcement and the Persistence of Behavior: Experimental Evidence*, SSRN Electronic Journal, July 2010

Mark T. Gilderhus Mark T., *History and Historians: A Historiographical Introduction*, Pearson, London, 2002

Habermas J., *The theory of communicative action*, Translated by Thomas McCarthy, Beacon Press, Boston, 1984

Hepper, E. G., Ritchie, T. D., Sedikides, C., & Wildschut, T., *Odyssey's end: Lay conceptions of nostalgia reflect its original homeric meaning*. Emotion, 12(1), 102–119. 2012 https://doi. org/10.1037/a0025167

Hughes, Simon Mark, *Automatic inference of causal reasoning chains from student essays* (2019). College of Computing and Digital Media Dissertations 19 Also [online] https://via.library. depaul.edu/cdm_etd/19 accessed 10/12/2020

Hume David, *An Enquiry Concerning Human Understanding*, Edited by Millican Peter, Oxford University Press, Oxford, 2007

Ibarra Herminia, Scoular Anne, *The Leader as Coach: How to unleash innovation, energy, and commitment*, Harvard Business Review, November-December 2019

Isenberg, D. J.. *How senior managers think*. Harvard Business Review, 62, 1984, 81–90.

Isenberg, D. J., *Thinking and managing: A verbal protocol analysis of managerial problem solving*. Academy of Management Journal, 4, 1986, 75–78.

Johnson , M.W., Christensen C.M., Kagermann H., *Reinventing Your Business Model*, Harvard Business Review, December 2008

Latour B. Science in Action: *How to Follow Scientists and Engineers through Society*, Harvard UniversityScience in Action How to Follow Scientists and Engineers through Society Press, Cambridge Ma., 1998

Locke John, Complete Works of John Locke, *An Essay Concerning Human Understanding, Book II Chapter XXXIII Section 17*, Delphi Classics, Hastings East Sussex, 2017

Kancel Chris, *Happy Brain Boost Your Dopamine, Serotonin, Oxytocin & Other Neurotransmitters Naturally, Improve Your Focus and Brain Functions*, Live & Life Publishing at KDP, 2016

Mendenhall William, Beaver Robert J. Beaver Barbara M. *Introduction to Probability and Statistics*, Fourteenth Edition, Brooks/Cole, Cengage Learning, Boston, 2013

Mintzberg H and Waters J.A., *Of strategies deliberate and emergent*, strategic management journal, Vol 6. 1985 Pp. 257-272

Mok Kimberly, *Artificial 'Imagination' Helped Google AI Master Go, the Most Complex Game Ever Invented,* The New Stack, Jan 31st, 2016, available at https://thenewstack.io/google-ai-beats-human-champion-complex-game-ever-invented/ accessed on 23/02/2024

Neisser, U. (1976). *General, academic, and artificial intelligence,* In L. Resnick (Ed.), *Human intelligence: Perspectives on its theory and measurement* (pp. 179–189). Norwood, N.J.: Ablex.

Patanakul, P., Chen J., Lynn, G., *Autonomous Teams and New Product Development*, Journal of Product Innovation Management, Sep 2012,, pp 734-750

Peirce S.C., *A General Introduction to the Semiotic*, Indiana University Press, Bloomington, 1996

Peduzzi P., Concato J., Kemper E., Holford T.R., Feinstein A.R., *A simulation study of the number of events per variable in logistic regression analysis*, Journal of Clinical Epidemiology, VOLUME 49, ISSUE 12, P1373-1379, DECEMBER 1996

Piaget J., *The language and thought of the child*, translated by Marjorie and Ruth Gabain, Routledge, London, 2005

Plata Serge, *Visions of Applied Mathematics*, Peter Lang, Oxford, 2007

Plata Serge, *Neural Networks are Homeomorphisms: An Introduction to Higher Mathematics for Decision Scientists*, Clapham Publishing Services, London, 2023

Plata Serge, Raczkiewvicz Magdalena, *A New Approach to Forecast Accuracy,* AI & Automation Business Journal, 2023, Vol 1, pp. 52-65, available at https://www.infosysconsultinginsights.com/insights/ai-automation-business-journal/ accessed on 9/3/2024

Plata Serge, Ioannou Jovana, *Go LIGHT with teams: The next level of implementation strategy*, available at https://blogs.infosys.com/infosys-consulting/management/go-light-with-teams-the-next-level-of-implementation-strategy.html accessed on 1/5/24

Poincare, H., *Science and Method*, Cosimo Classics, Shropshire, 2007

Popper K., *The logic of scientific Discovery*, Routledge Classics, London, 1992

Porter M.E. *Competitive advantage: Creating a sustaining superior performance*, New York Free Press, 1985

Powel Thomas, *Strategy as Diligence: Putting Behavioral Strategy into Practice*, California Management Review 2017, Vol. 59(3) 162–190

Ricoeur P., *Hermeneutics and the human science*, translated by John B. Thomson, Cambridge University Press, Cambridge UK, 1981

Ridley R., He L., Xinyu D., ShujianH, Jiajun C., *Prompt Agnostic Essay Scorer: A Domain Generalization Approach to Cross-prompt Automated Essay Scoring,* arXiv:2008.01441, August 2020

Riley R.D., Snell K.I., Ensor J., Burke D.L., Harrell F.E., Moons K.GM, Collins G.S., *Minimum sample size for developing a multivariable prediction model: PART II ⊠ binary and time⊠ to⊠event outcomes*, Statistics in Medicine, 2019 Mar 30; 38(7): 1276–1296.

Ritson Mark, *Marketers should pay more attention to attention*, Marketing Week, September 2022, available at https://www.marketingweek.com/ritson-pay-attention-to-attention/ accessed on 21/02/2024

Segal J., *Le zéro et le un Histoire de la notion d'information au XXe siècle*, Éditions Matériologiques, Paris, 2011

Simondon G, *On the mode of existence of technical objects*, translated by Cecile Malaspina and John Rogove, Univocal Publishing, Minneapolis, 2017

Smaller Barbara, *A Wife Speaks To Her Husband*, available at https://condenaststore.com/featured/a-wife-speaks-to-her-husband-barbara-smaller.html accessed 19/03/2024

Smith Adam, edited by Edwin Cannan, *An inquiry into the nature and causes of the wealth of nations*, University of Chicago Press, Chicago, 1977

Steiner G., *Real Presences*, University of Chicago Press; 2nd ed. Edition, Chicago, 1991

Stuart Mill John, *The complete works of John Stuart Mill, Utilitarianism*, Delphi Classics, Hastings East Sussex, 2019 Venturebit, 2019, https://venturebeat.com/2020/01/02/superdata-games-hit-120-1-billion-in-2019-with-fortnite-topping-1-8-billion/ accessed on 29/02/2024

Vittinghoff E., McCulloch C.E., *Relaxing the Rule of Ten Events per Variable in Logistic and Cox Regression,* American Journal of Epidemiology, Volume 165, Issue 6, 15 March 2007, Pages 710–718

Wagner, R. K., *Smart people doing dumb things: the case of managerial incompetence*, In Sternberg, R. K. (Ed.), *Why Smart People Can Be So Stupid*, New Haven, CT: Yale University Press, 42–63, 2002

Wagner, R. K., & R. J., *Practical intelligence in real-world pursuits: The role of tacit knowledge,* Journal of Personality and Social Psychology, 49, 436–458, 1985

Wiener N., *Cybernetics or control and communication in the animal and the machine*, The MIT Press, Cambridge Massachusetts, 1965

WIlkinson & FinkBeiner, *Divorce Statistics: Over 115 Studies, Facts and Rates For 2024*, 2024, available at https://www.wf-lawyers.com/divorce-statistics-and-facts/, accessed on 20/03/2024

World line.svg, SVG version: K. Aainsqatsi at en.wikipedia Original PNG version: Stib at en.wikipedia - Transferred from en.wikipedia to Commons. (Original text: self-made) SVG version of Image:World_line.png, CC BY-SA 3.0, File:World line. svg, Created: 7 May 2007, Uploaded: 18 April 2020

Wynee, Jessica, *Do Not Erase: Mathematicians and Their Chalkboards*, Princeton University Press, Princeton, 2021

Zhang H., Magooda A., Litman D., Correnti R., Wang E.,Matsmura L.C., Howe E., Quintana R., *eRevise: Using Natural Language Processing to Provide Formative Feedback on Text Evidence Usage in Student Writing*, Proceedings of the AAAI Conference on Artificial Intelligence (August 2019) vol. 33, 9619-9625